Tax Guide 202

BEFORE STARTING A BUSINESS

by

Holmes F. Crouch
Tax Specialist

D1523165

Published by

Allyear Tax Guides
20484 Glen Brae Drive
Saratoga, CA 95070

ISBN 0944817793

LCCN 2006920395

Printed in U.S.A.

Series 200
Investors & Businesses

Tax Guide 202

BEFORE STARTING A BUSINESS

For other titles in print, see page 224.

The author: **Holmes F. Crouch**
For more about the author, see page 221.

PREFACE

If you are a knowledge-seeking **taxpayer** looking for information, this book can be helpful to you. It is designed to be read — from cover to cover — in about eight hours. Or, it can be "skim-read" in about 30 minutes.

Either way, you are treated to **tax knowledge** . . . *beyond the ordinary*. The "beyond" is that which cannot be found in IRS publications, the IRS web site, IRS e-file instructions, or tax software programs.

Taxpayers have different levels of interest in a selected subject. For this reason, this book starts with introductory fundamentals and progresses onward. You can verify the progression by chapter and section in the table of contents. In the text, "applicable law" is quoted in pertinent part. Key phrases and key tax forms are emphasized. Real-life examples are given . . . in down-to-earth style.

This book has 12 chapters. This number provides depth without cross-subject rambling. Each chapter starts with a head summary of meaningful information.

To aid in your skim-reading, informative diagrams and tables are placed strategically throughout the text. By leafing through page by page, reading the summaries and section headings, and glancing at the diagrams and tables, you can get a good handle on the matters covered.

Effort has been made to update and incorporate all of the latest tax law changes that are *significant* to the title subject. However, "beyond the ordinary" does not encompass every conceivable variant of fact and law that might give rise to protracted dispute and litigation. Consequently, if a particular statement or paragraph is crucial to your own specific case, you are urged to seek professional counseling. Otherwise, the information presented is general and is designed for a broad range of reader interests.

The Author

INTRODUCTION

You see an attention-grabbing business advertisement. It blares at you, saying—

> *Form your own corporation; Be your own CEO; Pay yourself a 6-figure salary; Charge your personal, family, and living expenses to the corporation; Pay no corporation income tax; Be protected from lawsuits — all for the one low price of $500 for our easy-to-follow 'Corporation Kit.' Act now!*

Many a would-be entrepreneur has been caught off guard by illusory inferences of fame and fortune — and no tax — if one simply incorporates out of state or offshore. If you believe in fairy tales, dream on. Follow your fantasy . . . until, one day, you come back down to earth.

When you do, there is a lot of prebusiness reality to engage in. For example, all of that money that is gong to come gushing in. What do you do with that money? How do you categorize it? Does any of it belong to employees as withholdings? Is any of it sales tax collections? Is any of it borrowed money (from family, friends, bank)? Is any of it "investor" money (who'll be watching you like a hawk)? Sooner or later, you will have to account for all of this money. Some will be tax collections that have to be forked over to federal and state agencies. Some will be returned to customers, clients, lenders, and investors. And some will represent profit . . . subject, of course, to tax. This is where our Chapter 5: *Bank Deposits Discipline*, comes in handy.

We have other chapters also. We present definitional terms, what constitutes startup costs, types of businesses, cost of goods sold, amortization and depreciation rules, preparing for tax audits, and compensation of owners.

You have a choice in the *form* of business that you start with. You can choose to be a proprietorship, a partnership (general or limited), an LLC (Limited Liability Company), an S corporation, or a C corporation. Each form has its advantages and disadvantages. We'll explain the differences herein.

You'll need to select one form of business, at least initially. You can always change at any time. Whatever form you choose, however, should not be done based on any misperceived tax or legal liability benefits. As the business owner, you are always liable for the tax misdeeds and mismanagement activities that take place during your watch.

Other than gross mismanagement, tax mismanagement is one of the greatest causes of new business failures. Many a new business has been abruptly shut down by the IRS. Most of these shutdowns are for failure to file employer tax returns, and/or for failure to withhold and pay (to the IRS) quarterly income tax withholdings, social security taxes, medicare taxes, and federal unemployment taxes. We devote a whole chapter to these employer/employee tax matters. What we are trying to tell you now is that tax matters should be among your foremost investigatory concerns when preparing to start any new business.

One of your first tax-matter concerns should be: "What do I do about startup costs?" As we all know, starting any new business requires certain up-front expenditures. One must spend money for investigating, creating, and bringing into operation an active trade or business. Taxwise, how do you handle these up-front, out-of-pocket expenditures?

Answer: You may *elect* to deduct up to $5,000 as startup expenditures in the year in which your business commences. All expenditures in excess of this amount must be collected, totaled, and amortized over 15 years. Your venture-capitalist investors (and lenders) are not going to like this.

There are many other "Before Starting Business" matters that you should investigate. This being a tax book, we focus primarily on tax concerns and business entity forms. We leave to others product research, development of services, marketing and sales, and the solicitation of operational funds.

Taxwise, you are not in business until the first dollar of income is derived from a product or service you offer to the general public. And, following this first dollar, there must be some expectation that your business will be ongoing and active. From this point on, you are "in business."

CONTENTS

1

PROFIT MOTIVE FACTORS

> For Every Trade Or Business, There Is A "Silent Partner" - The IRS - Who Sets The Tax Rules Of Operation. Foremost Is A Profit Motivation With Material Participation By The Owner(s) Therein. Specifically, There Are NINE OBJECTIVE FACTORS (Among Others) Which The IRS Weighs. Otherwise, Not-For-Profit Rules And Passive Activity Rules Come Into Play. Having More Than One Business Is Tax Suspect If One Is Successful And Others Are Not. Until Your New Business Is Active And Ongoing, It Is A "Nonbusiness." Meanwhile, Segregate Your Startup Costs Into Two Categories: Amortizeable And Depreciable.

Before starting any business, there is one reality of life you must endure. Without your permission, you have a *silent partner* to please. Even though such partner contributes no money, no expertise, and no management skills to your endeavor, it has some say in how you run the business, and in how you account for its monies IN and monies OUT. You surely know whom we are referring to, namely: the Internal Revenue Service — **the IRS**!

Do not take this silent partner matter too seriously. In particular, do not be paranoid about it. The IRS is simply a tax monitoring agency that has been mandated by Congress to assure that you are truly profit motivated — based on nine objective factors — and to assure that your startup costs are not written off prematurely. You are not actively in business until you make some profit more or less regularly.

Otherwise, you are free to dream up and activate your "business plan" in any manner you see fit. Although many bright ideas can form in your mind, only those which culminate in an active trade or business are recognized for tax purposes. If a new business never comes to fruition, all expenditures therewith are treated as nondeductible personal expenses. They are "personal" because they originate in your mind. They are "nondeductible" because there is no business income against which such expenditures can be offset.

It is important, therefore, that we touch on certain IRS matters that you should know about before your business gets going. To do so, we will focus more on how the Internal Revenue Code (IRC) looks at your business rather than on what your business plan should be. There are others who can better assist you with that plan than we. Our realm pertains to tax matters and to the tax recognition of your business. In this regard, we start with selected tax-related definitional terms.

"Trade or Business" Defined

Throughout the Internal Revenue Code, the phrase "trade or business" appears frequently. This raises the logical question: What is a trade or business? How is it defined?

In essence, a trade or business is an activity carried on for profit. Underlying everything else, there must be a true and genuine profit-seeking motive. While there can never be a guarantee of profit, there must be a reasonable expectation of earning one, under ordinary market conditions. If the profit motive is lacking, the activity is a not-for-profit endeavor. Such endeavors are not tax recognized.

Tax recognition arises from the fact that when a profit is made, there are taxes to be paid. The IRS simply will not recognize your business unless there is government revenue to be derived. Some leeway is permitted in the early years of startup.

Associated with the profit motive of a business, is the earning of a livelihood by the owner or owners thereof. One cannot earn a livelihood if the business loses money year after year. Therefore, when a profit is made, there are taxes to pay. The after-tax profit is thus available for sustaining the livelihood and well-being of the entrepreneur(s) involved.

A profit is made when a product or service is offered on an ongoing basis. The term "ongoing" means: day-to-day, month-to-month, year-to-year. In other words, a one-time profit does not constitute a business. More likely than not, a one-time profit is an investment, a wager, a hobby, a recreation, or other personal transaction. To be recognized as a trade or business, the profit must be made on a continuing and repeated basis. In the continuum process, some of the transactions may be made at a profit, and some may be made at a loss. The vicissitudes of the marketplace determine the net profitability . . . or net loss.

Another feature of a trade or business is the offering of your product or service to the general public. While the form of ownership may be private, the business must be open to the public at large. Family members, close friends, business associates, and others in exclusionary groupings do not constitute the general public. While a net profit may indeed be made from such persons, the transactions are suspect. This is because the element of competition is lacking.

At this point, we have described four essential features that characterize a trade or business (for tax purposes). There is a fifth feature — material participation — that we must tell you about separately. This one feature alone is key.

Material Participation Required

Over the years, Congress passed many tax laws affecting large and small businesses. Some of the laws are "anti" business in the sense that they redefine what a trade or business is. A particular law on point is Section 469: *Passive Activity Losses Limited*. In essence, Section 469 classifies a trade or business into two categories. These two categories are (1) a *passive activity* business, and (2) a *material participation* business.

A passive activity business is one in which the conduct of the owner(s) does not qualify it as a material participation business. The passive activity owner(s) are overseers and investors. They are more interested in the generation of tax benefits rather than in the day-to-day operation of the business. Any discussion of passive activity businesses is beyond the scope of this book. Our focus is solely on material participation businesses.

A material participation business is one in which the owner or owners are involved in the business operations on a regular, continuous, and substantial basis. This level of participation must be maintained throughout the tax year. Included in this feature is participation of the owner's spouse, where appropriate. A husband and wife in business together are treated as one taxpayer.

A taxpayer is most likely to have participated where his own involvement is his principal activity. In other words, his primary income depends on the success of the business. By contrast, a full-time lawyer or doctor who invests in an orange grove is unlikely to have materially participated in the orange grove business. Their money participates, but not their persons.

A "highly relevant" factor is how regularly you as owner are present at the place where your principal business operations are carried on. Full-time involvement is not necessary if the nature of the business is seasonal, or where qualified employees and independent contractors perform designated routine and special tasks. In other words, being at your place of business 8 to 10 hours each day is not crucial. You are materially participating if you do everything that is required to conduct and control the business.

To summarize where we are at this point, we present Figure 1.1. We identify therein the five key elements for gaining tax recognition as a trade or business. But, as we will see below, even full compliance with Figure 1.1 provides no tax guarantees.

The Not-for-Profit Presumption

Government always has a lot to say about how you run your business. It can't run its own affairs properly, but it can tell you how to run yours. As far as profit-making is concerned, the government — via the IRS — says that you must make a profit in any three out of five consecutive years that you are in business. If you do not make such a profit, it is *presumed* that you are engaged in a not-for-profit activity.

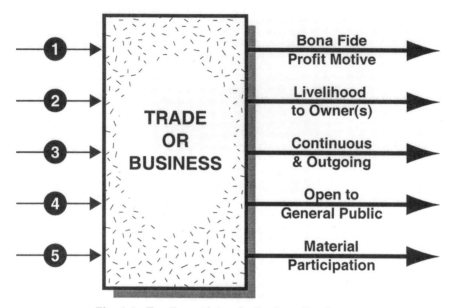

Fig. 1.1 - Tax Essentials of a Trade or Business

This is all spelled out in tax code Section 183: *Activities Not Engaged in for Profit*. The essence of this tax law is that—

In the case of an activity . . . not engaged in for profit, no deduction attributable to such activity shall be allowed . . . except . . . to the extent [of] the gross income derived from such activity for the taxable year.

Let us exemplify what this means. Suppose that the gross income from your business is $10,000 for the year. To derive this amount, you actually spent $30,000. According to Section 183, you have a $20,000 personal loss that is not recognized. It is a "loss-loss" . . . meaning no writeoffs whatsoever.

This is the old familiar story encountered by experienced persons in business. If the flip of a coin comes up "heads" — the government wins. If it comes up "tails" — the government also wins. In either case, it is a loss-loss to you.

The teeth of Section 183 are found in subsection (d): *Presumption*. This subsection reads in part—

If the gross income derived from an activity for 3 or more of the taxable years in the period of 5 consecutive taxable years . . . exceeds the deductions attributable to such activity . . . then, unless the [IRS] establishes to the contrary, such activity shall be presumed . . . to be an activity engaged in for profit.

Thus, the reverse presumption is that, if you do not make a profit in three out of five years, you are some kind of flake trying to rip off the government. As a tax "presumption," however, you can refute this anti-business stance of the IRS.

In more specific terms, IRS Regulation 1.183-2(a) says—

*For purposes of Section 183 . . . the term "activity not engaged in for profit" means any activity . . . carried on primarily as a sport, hobby, or for recreation. The determination . . . is to be made by reference to objective standards, taking into account all of the facts and circumstances of each case. Although a reasonable expectation of profit is not required, the facts and circumstances must indicate that the taxpayer entered into the activity, or continued the activity, **with the objective of making a profit**. [Emphasis supplied.]*

So the key for distinguishing between for-profit and not-for-profit is the *objective* of making a profit. In determining whether this objective exists, the amount of profit is immaterial. Whether small or large, the objective exists if there is a reasonable chance of making some profit. Greater weight is given to objective facts than to one's mere statement of intent.

Nine Objective Factors

Not many businesses make a significant profit in the first few years of operation. Startup losses are the rule rather than the exception. Consequently, the first few years of a new trade or business are the most vulnerable to IRS attack. This is particularly true if the loss claimant has other sources of positive income.

In Regulation 1.183-2(b), the IRS has set forth nine different relevant factors for determining whether a business is operated for profit. These nine factors are identified in Figure 1.2. Note that a thumbnail description of each factor is presented. We also show checkboxes for entering "Yes" or "No" when reviewing your own business activity. A "Yes" means for profit whereas a "No" means not-for-profit.

The listing in Figure 1.2 is not all inclusive. Depending on the particular business that you envision, there may be other factors that should be considered. No one factor is determinative by itself.

The manner of carrying on a business (Factor 1 in Figure 1.2) is certainly one good indication of the "Yes" or "No" profit motive. If the owner carries on his affairs in a businesslike manner, and he keeps complete and accurate books and records, he certainly has a profit objective in mind. Similarly, where an activity is carried on in a manner comparable to competitive activities of the same nature that are profitable, a profit motive may be (often is) indicated.

On the other hand, if there are elements of personal pleasure or recreation that stand out (Factor 9 in Figure 1.2), a not-for-profit objective is suspected. Apparently, one is not supposed to enjoy or like his work. The inference is that one must work with the exclusive intention of deriving a profit . . . and maximizing it. However, the fact that one does derive some personal pleasure from his business is not, in and of itself, determinative, if the for-profit objective is evidenced by other factors.

More Than One Business

Having more than one business tends to be tax suspect. This is especially true where one business is highly successful and the other is not. The passive loss rules and the not-for-profit rules both come into play.

For example, suppose you own and run business A and business B. Business A is highly successful: your net profit is $100,000 year after year. But business B is a loser. Its net loss year after year is <$35,000>. As the common owner of both businesses, you can net-net the $100,000 profit with the <$35,000> loss. This gives you a taxable net of $65,000. In a situation like this, you can be sure that — at some point in time — business B will be tax scrutinized.

Tax Test	ITEM	DESCRIPTION	Yes	No
1	Manner of conducting business	Businesslike with complete and accurate records; changing un- profitable methods and improving operations.		
2	Expertise of owner and advisors	Adequate preparation, research, study, and followthrough with sound "business plan"; pursuing new products and services.		
3	Time and effort expended by owners	Devotion of much time and energy to an activity where personal and recreational aspects are minimal.		
4	Expectation of growth and appreciation	Current profits not determinative if prospects of business growth and appreciation of assets are realistic.		
5	Success in other similar activities	Prior business success and turn- arounds indicative of profit making intent in current business.		
6	History of losses and reasons therefore	Continued losses must be ex- plainable in terms of risks, reverses, unforeseens, and de- pressed markets.		
7	Occasionality of profits: some large, some small	With large capital involved, irreg- ular profits indicate speculative venture with chance to make big.		
8	Other sources of income	If primary income from current activity: good; if substantial other income: bad.		
9	Elements of personal pleasure or recreation	Particularly suspect are activities involving sports, hobbies, enter- tainment, collector items, exotic pets, and prestigiousness.		

Fig. 1.2 - Factors Indicating a "For Profit" Activity

There is nothing inherently wrong with having two, three, or more businesses. Nor is there anything wrong with one or more being successful, and one or more being unsuccessful. That is, there is nothing wrong so long as there is a clear business purpose and rationale for each business. Each business should be a separate economic unit, separately managed with separate record-keeping, and targeting separate segments of the marketplace.

Where there is common ownership of more than one business, the test of *economic reality* applies. Do the separate businesses complement each other in a seasonal and functional manner, which makes good business sense? Or, does one of them appear to be a "front" or tax shelter for the main business of the owner(s)? Is there a large loss in the same year as a large profit?

Here's an example of economic reality involving three separate businesses. You and your spouse own a motel that produces good net income. The peak season, however, is June through September, which is four months of the year. What do you do during the eight months of off-season?

Suppose you have background and training in commercial advertising. You start an advertising business whose peak season is October through January (four months). Suppose your spouse has a background in geography and travel. She starts a small travel agency whose peak season for bookings and reservations is February through May (four months). Together, you have three separate businesses. Each is a separate economic unit; each offers a different product or service; and each has a separate niche in the marketplace. Nothing is tax-wrong with this at all . . . providing you keep *separate* books and records for each business.

On the other hand, suppose you inherit a large farm, but you work in the city on a full-time basis. You pay someone to manage and run the farm. As most farms do, it produces a loss year after year. Now, farming is a perfectly legitimate business for one who indeed "works the land." Since you don't work the land, you are a gentleman farmer. Gentleman farming is not a trade or business. Hence, the not-for-profit rules apply.

Methods & Phases of "Starting"

What is a new business, and when does it start? It is "new" in the sense that you as the owner have never operated that business before. It "starts" when you are prepared to follow through on your first public offering of a product or service . . . which is accepted. Up to the point where an active/ongoing enterprise begins to take shape, you are *not* in business.

One can start a new business in any of several ways. You can start from scratch. You can inherit a business or gradually buy into one. You can revive a defunct business. You can acquire a business by purchase or by franchising. Or, you can spin off a new business from an existing business in which you have participated.

Rather than discussing each of the ways of getting started, we present a brief summary of their pros and cons in Figure 1.3. Our position is that no matter how you actually get started, there is a prebusiness phase of thinking and planning. You just don't jump into business overnight . . . and make millions of dollars.

For any of the starting methods in Figure 1.3, there are five stages of entry progression. In sequential order, these stages are:

I — The Prerequisite Stage

• You must have some prior knowledge, experience, background or training in the new business line that you expect to engage in. You should also have some foreknowledge of the specific product(s) and/or service(s) that you intend to offer, in your target domain.

II — The Idea Formulation Stage

• An incubation period of reading, talking, thinking, and investigating the new venture that you are about to embark on; the idea needs to become a reality in your mind and not just a passing dream. To test your idea, engage in informal discussions with prospective customers, clients, and your friends.

III — The Paper Plan Stage

• Here is where you write it all down: charts, diagrams, and outlines; you define your "business objectives": your product or service, marketing strategy, "marketing plan," production and/or supply sources, and the organizational personnel that you will need.

	METHOD	PROS	CONS
1	Inheriting from parent(s) or close family	Established product, service, market, & clients; long track record of earnings; ongoing goodwill makes take-over easy.	Long "estate transfer" period; product/service may be out-of-date; inheritor may be disinterested in continuing the business.
2	Buying (or buying into) existing business	Good growth potential if business on sound footing; saves trial and error; earnings record & marketing can be examined.	Might just be buying prior owners' problems; all facts may not be fully disclosed; probably near defunct or near retirement.
3	Franchising into a national product or service	Proven product or service line "nationally advertised"; management training provided; products delivered without credit hassle.	Large amount of entry capital needed; franchisor may set unrealistic sales goals; difficult to change product or service line.
4	"Spin-off" from successful larger business	Long "incubation time" to assess new product/service; some financial assistance; temporary sharing of facilities.	Requires covenants "not-to-compete"; covenants against "raiding" of personnel; potential lawsuits over patent and market infringments.
5	Starting new from scratch; "boot-strapping"	If unique product or service, can be highly satisfying; complete ownership and control; no covenants or prior lines to continue.	Initial "floundering" can be costly; endangered competition can be ruthless; repeat customers & clients slow to develop.

Fig. 1.3 - Ways of Getting Started in Business

IV — The Earnest Money Stage

• Up-front money has to be expended for inventory, materials, supplies, equipment, rental space, utilities, consultants, and contractors; who will advance this money . . . and how much is needed?

V — The Launching Stage

• Detailed preparatory effort in the form of contracts, commitments, advertising, promotion, name recognition, address, hours of operation, and so on; guarantee of delivery and follow-through.

Stages I through III should be on a very low budget. The planning and formulation of a new business idea requires more time and thought than it does money. Doing things on paper is much cheaper than doing them in fact. Beginner mistakes can be made which can be corrected before serious money is committed. Research, phone calls, and perhaps a short trip or two, are not high-cost items. Absorb these costs in your personal budget. Don't even bother to keep record of them. They are — or should be — rather trivial when compared to the costs in Stages IV and V.

Startup Costs Defined

In the sequential listing above, stages IV and V are where the serious money is needed. Every proposed venture has to undergo some prebusiness expenditures to bring the concept into a form conducive to public acceptance. Make sure that you have enough money and resources to do this. Most new businesses fail at this point (called: *undercapitalization*). At this point, also, serious recordkeeping must commence.

The costs in stages IV and V can be segregated into two classifications: *intangible* costs and *tangible* costs. Intangible costs are those incurred for the investigative, creative, organizational, consultative, and promotional aspects of getting a business going. Tangible costs, on the other hand, are those incurred for the acquisition of vehicles, machinery, equipment, furniture, and fixtures — physical assets — to be used in the business. Separate recordkeeping should be maintained for each of these two classes of expenditures.

Tax code Section 195(c) defines "startup expenditures" as—

Any amount . . . paid or incurred in connection with—

(i) investigating the creation or acquisition of an active trade or business, or

(ii) creating an active trade or business, or
(iii)any activity engaged in for profit and for the production of income before the day on which the active trade or business begins.

If you read this section carefully, you will see that no distinction is made between intangible (nonphysical) and tangible (physical) costs. You are left out on a limb. Section 195(c) is trying to tell you just one thing. All expenditures incurred before a business actually begins must be accumulated separately from the business itself. If the intended business never gets going, these accumulated costs are not tax recognized. No income has been generated against which they can be deducted.

If your business indeed gets going, then the distinction between intangible and tangible costs becomes important. Intangible costs can be amortized (Sec. 195(b); tangible costs can be depreciated (Sec. 167(a)). We will reserve to the next chapter all discussion on amortization and depreciation. These become "spread-out" deductions against the income of the active business.

Simplified Cost Accumulation

Very few new businesses actually start up and get going within a given tax year. Usually, two, three, or more preparatory years are involved. During this time, you will be incurring costs that have no immediate benefit to you. Chances are, you'll become cavalier. You'll either try to write them off against other sources of income, or you may overlook them altogether.

You may even have several new business ideas in your mind all at one time. Your style may be to trial-and-error each one until one of them clicks. Obviously, you need some sort of systematic cost accumulation system.

The minute you start spending real money, we urge that you establish a "business startup" checking account. Do this at the financial institution of your choice. Use your personal name and the personal name(s) of your associate(s). Do not use any fictitious name or any prospective business name. Up to the point where your prospective business actually goes into operation, all of the expenditures are essentially personal.

What is "real money" to justify setting up a separate startup checking account? That depends on the nature and capital requirements of your proposed business. Certainly, if your cumulative costs begin to exceed $1,000, you should open the separate account. Then feed personal money into this account in $1,000 to $10,000 increments, as needed. The deposit confirmation slips become third-party records as to whose personal money was deposited, and how much. Forget about interest on the deposits. The startup account is not for personal savings; it is simply a cost accumulation check-writing system.

We now suggest a really neat feature to you. Have the financial institution print *two* different types of checks: different colors with different imprint designs. Use the same account number and personal names on both checks. All you want is to be able to make a quick eye-distinction between the two check forms. Call one your "A" checks and the other your "B" checks.

Use the "A" checks for your intangible cost expenditures and the "B" checks for your tangible costs (physical assets). Having two types of checks forces you to think, on the spot, in terms of intangible/tangible expenditures. Whether you accumulate your costs over several months or several years, this is all the startup tax accounting that you need. Keep your startup life simple. The scheme that we have in mind is depicted in Figure 1.4.

When your business finally gets going, you total up all the "A" checks and enter that amount on your tax form amortization schedule. As to the "B" checks, you may have to subcategorize them into vehicles, machinery, equipment, furniture, and fixtures, before entering them on your tax form depreciation schedule.

Timing When to be "In Business"

Every business activity has its own cyclic characteristics: its good months and low months. Consequently, before you execute your "launching experience," find out about the seasonal aspects of the business that you are about to enter. Talk to your competition (in a friendly manner); talk to friends who are acquainted with the type of business you envision; and talk to potential customers and clients and ascertain their buying habits. Try to determine the best three to five consecutive months of the new business. Keep in mind that you are gauging the "profit potential" even if only for a 3-to-5-month period.

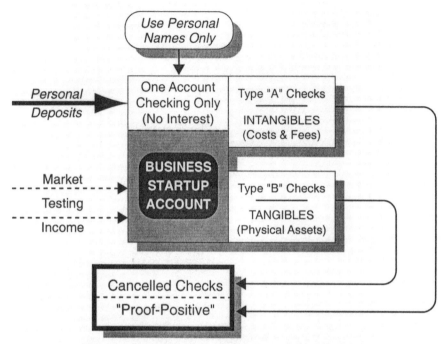

Fig. 1.4 - Two-Check Accumulation of Startup Costs

You have spent a wad of personal money getting ready. Do not blow it by coming on line off-season. Nor do you want to get in at the very beginning of the next buying season. Existing competition already has the name recognition that you do not have. Do not intentionally lock horns with them. Make sure that you are truly probing a new niche.

The ideal entry timing is approximately one-third of the way into the peak cycle of your intended year. Most customers and clients buy late in the cycle, rather than early. The early buyers habitually go back to their old sources, and rarely try anything new. The mid- and late-cycle buyers are your best chance. Many small businesses have a three-to-five-month spread of intense activity, followed by seven to nine months that are slow. In Figure 1.5, we present our depiction of some likely income profiles.

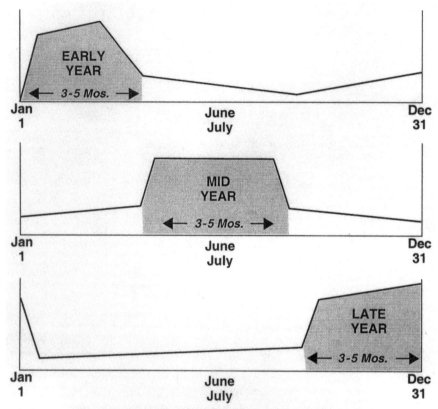

Fig. 1.5 - Likely "Income Profile" of a Small Business

Ideally, you'd like to have a few months after the business cycle wanes to review your launch experience. You want time to critique the affair before you make irreversible decisions. If things look good enough to declare that you are in business, you want time to clean up your act before getting locked into a tax bureaucracy and computer-intimidation system that is difficult to get out of.

During the three-to-five-months' trial experience, there will be income and expenses. If your income exceeds your expenses, you are probably in business. If your expenses exceed income, you have probably made a "market test." If a market test, the excess expenses are treated as startup costs. These market-testing costs simply add to the cost accumulation system that we presented back in Figure 1.4.

2

DEFERRED CAPITAL RECOVERY

To Get Any Type Of Business Going, UPFRONT CAPITAL Must Be Expended. If Creating A Business, There Are Startup Costs; If Taking One Over, There Are Acquisition Costs. In Either Case, There Are Capital Outlays For Vehicles, Machinery, Equipment, Tools, And Structures. You Need To Acquire/Create "Things" In Order To Produce, Sell, And Service "Things." Your Recovery (Or Return) Of This Capital Is NOT Immediate; It Is Deferred Over Numerous YEARS. Except For The "Section 179 Election To Expense" (Up To $100,000), Your Capital Cost Recovery Period Is Set By Special Tax Rules For AMORTIZATION And DEPRECIATION.

There is one class of before starting business expenditures which — sometimes — is hard to explain to first-timers in business. The class to which we refer is called *capital expenditures*. They are "capital" in the sense that they have *retained value* at the end of the first tax year of operation. They also have retained value (which diminishes) at the end of the second, third . . . fifth . . . tenth . . . or higher tax year. Because the items acquired by the expenditures are not fully consumed at the end of the first tax year, any deductions for the capital expended are prorated over a specified period of years. This is unlike operating expenditures for items and services which are fully consumed within the acquisition year.

There is the typical entrepreneurial reaction to the spread-out of cost recovery allowances for capital expenditures. The reaction goes like this: "If I incur upfront a legitimate capital expenditure for business purposes, I should be entitled to an immediate tax deduction for it. Why do I have to stretch my cost recovery out over time? I have to spend the money now. Yet, you tell me that I can't get an immediate deduction for it! Why not?"

We've already told you why not. You spend upfront $50,000 for a piece of machinery that will produce widgets for you over the next 10 years. At the end of seven years, say, it still has a useful life (and value) of three years. You spend the same $50,000 for an engineering consultant whose services are performed all in one year. The $50,000 machinery expenditure is recoverable in 10 years, whereas the $50,000 of consulting expense is recoverable in the year of performance. Do you get the distinction?

The expenditures to which we are devoting this chapter, therefore, are recoverable as *amortization* and *depreciation*. These are special — and peculiar — tax rules called: "capital cost recovery (deduction) rules." We want to tell you about them. They are equally applicable to all forms of business, whether proprietorship, partnership, LLC (Limited Liability Company), S corporation, or C corporation. They are also equally applicable to all types of businesses, whether manufacturing, sales, service, farming, or the extraction of natural resources.

What is Amortization?

Amortization is a term that many taxpayers have seen and used, rather automatically. Although frequently used, its tax significance is not always understood.

Amortization is a uniform deduction that applies primarily to the cost of *creating* certain intangibles in a trade or business. The act of creating derives within, by, for, or from each particular business. As such, the created asset is not an item that is ordinarily purchased on the retail market. It is rare that any amortizable items of cost pre-exist the business to which they relate. Hence, the key distinguishing feature of amortization is creativity . . . rather than purchasability.

In the Introduction to the book, we gave you (perhaps) the best example of the creation of an amortizable asset. The example directed your attention to the startup expenditures of your new business. We told you then that your startup costs were not immediately tax deductible.

As we explained in Chapter 1, startup consists of those intangible costs incurred for the investigation, creation, organizing, consulting, and promoting the idea of a new business. The costs are accumulated — held in suspense — until the business actually gets going. These costs are indigenous to your one business alone. We stressed the accumulation aspects of these costs in Figure 1.4.

There are other examples of the creation of amortizable costs. Among these are organizational and expansion costs, lease and lease modification costs, covenants not to compete, research and development costs, circulation expenditures, market research costs, prepaid insurance contracts, points and fees for business loans, business licenses and franchises, examination and appraisal fees, rehabilitation expenditures, mining exploration and development costs, and many others. All have in common the feature of creativity: one-of-a-kind for each particular business.

Once a business owner has created an amortizable asset, he is allowed — under certain conditions — to take an annual tax deduction against his cumulative costs. To get the deduction, however, four conditions must be met. These conditions are—

One. The amortization deduction must be statutorily allowed. One cannot accumulate costs of choice and amortize them at will.

Two. The amortization deduction must be expressly elected. It is not an automatic deduction as in the case of day-to-day (current) operating expenses. If not expressly elected, it has to be "capitalized." (We'll explain this later.)

Three. The amortization period must be prescribed either by statute or by an enforceable contract. One cannot select a period of his choice. The period must be greater than one year.

Four. The rate of amortization must be uniform and constant (straight line) month to month over the prescribed period. There can be no variation (no acceleration; no deceleration) to match the business income and its cycles.

If a business does not survive the amortization period, the unamortized costs are tax deductible in full, at the time the business ceases. Otherwise, the idea behind amortization is to prorate certain costs over the income-producing life of the business. This proration is designed so that there is no abnormal distortion to net taxable income. This, in principle, is the tax theory. Hence, recovering all of your legitimate capital expenditures for business is *deferred.*

The 15-Year Amortizations

Amortization is one of those "you can — but you can't" types of deduction that pervade the federal tax laws. You can take the deduction if it is statutorily sanctioned, but you can't take it (even if sanctioned) if you don't elect to do so properly and timely. In the background of every deferred recovery law is the desire by the IRS to capitalize/suspend the deduction on whatever pretext it can. Your only defense is to cite a specific applicable statute.

For illustrative citation purposes, there are four amortization laws that, at the very minimum, you should know about. There are many more than this number in the tax code — about 15 to 20 or so. The four that we have chosen are:

Sec. 195   — Start-Up Expenditures [proprietorships creation]

Sec. 197   — Goodwill and Other Intangibles [acquisition of an existing business]

Sec. 248   — Organizational Expenditures [for corporations]

Sec. 709   — Organization and Syndication Fees [for creation of partnerships and LLCs]

All four of these amortization statutes have in common a 15-year capital cost recovery period. Section 248 pertains to corporations whereas Section 709 pertains to partnerships. Otherwise, the statutory language of Sections 248 and 709 is virtually identical to that of Section 195.

Subsection 195(a) is subcaptioned: *Capitalization of Expenditures*. It reads—

Except as otherwise provided in this section, no deduction shall be allowed for start-up expenditures.

In other words, if Section 195 is not cited where applicable, all startup and related costs are "capitalized." This means that such costs become part of your *tax basis* in the business created or acquired. One's tax basis in property is recoverable only at the time the business is sold, exchanged, or terminated.

Subsection 195(b): ***Election to Deduct***, allows a deduction if you *elect* its provisions. If you do so, you—

*. . . shall be allowed a deduction for the taxable year in which the active trade or business begins in an amount equal to the **lesser of**—*
*(i)   the [actual] amount of start-up expenditures . . . **or***
*(ii) $5,000, reduced (but not below zero) by the amount by which the start-up expenditures exceed $50,000, **and***
the remainder [over $5,000] . . . shall be allowed as a deduction ratably over the 180-month period [15 years] beginning with the month in which the active trade or business begins [opens its doors to the public].

In other words, if you can create a business for $5,000 or less, you can expense those costs in the first year of operation. Otherwise, you must amortize your capital costs over a 15-year period. In the case of Section 197: ***Amortization of Goodwill***, etc., there is no $5,000 expensing opportunity. All costs of acquiring a "Section 197 Intangible" . . . *shall be amortized ratably over the 15-year period beginning with the month in which such intangible was acquired.* There are some 2,000 statutory words describing what a Section 197 intangible is. Included are such items as (1) workforce in place, (2) business books and records, (3) any patent, copyright, or formula, (4) any license or permit, (5) any covenant not to compete, (6) customer lists, (7) vendor contracts, (8) leasehold contracts . . . etc., etc.

There is a clear inference from the above four amortization statutes: Sections 195, 197, 247, and 709. Whether you create or acquire a business, whether in proprietorship, partnership, or corporate form, your initial capital costs are tax recoverable over

15 years. No passive investor or venture capitalist will tolerate this long a period. Therefore, as the entrepreneur of the business you must provide these initial costs out of your own pocket. A target "pocket amount" we suggest is $50,000. Relying solely on your skills to bootstrap a business with zero initial capital will not work.

How to Elect Amortization

For a new business entrepreneur, there are other amortization rules than those above that could be useful. There is Section 173: Circulation Expenditures, Section 174: Research and Experimental Expenditures, Section 175: Soil and Water Conservation Expenditures, Section 178: Cost of Acquiring a Lease, Section 194: Reforestation Expenditures, Section 616: Development Expenditures, Section 617: Certain Mining Exploration Expenditures, . . . and others. All of these tax code sections permit full recovery of one's capital in less than 15 years. The range of these recovery periods is 3, 5, 7, and 10 years.

The question now arises: How does one elect to amortize his applicable costs, instead of capitalizing them? The answer lies in Part VI of Form 4562. This IRS form is titled: ***Depreciation and Amortization.*** It is used by all entrepreneurial endeavors: proprietorships, partnerships, LLCs, S corporations, and C corporations. The election is made in the first year, in the first month of which the amortizable activity begins.

Once the activity begins, the election is made by entering six columns of information in Part VI: ***Amortization*** of Form 4562. See Figure 2.1 for the arrangement of this portion of Form 4562. The official captions for the six columns (which we shortened in Figure 2.1) are:

Col. (a) — *Description of costs*
Col. (b) — *Date amortization begins*
Col. (c) — *Amortizable amount*
Col. (d) — *Code section*
Col. (e) — *Amortization period or percentage*
Col. (f) — *Amortization for this year*

The horizontal lines in Figure 2.1 direct your attention to—

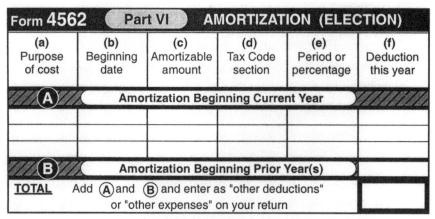

Fig. 2.1 - Information for Electing the Amortization Deduction

[1]   Amortization of costs that begins *during* your current tax year (after your business has started).
[2]   Amortization of costs that began *before* your current tax year.
[3]   *Total.* Add amounts in column (f) and report as "Other deductions" or "Other expenses" on the applicable schedule or form of your tax return.

Your amortization begins the moment the activity for which you expended capital begins productively. If the activity begins on August 16, say, you amortize for four months of that year. If the activity begins on August 15, you can amortize for five months. If the activity starts on or before the 15th of a month, you are allowed a full month. You divide the amount in column (c) by the number of months in column (e) to obtain the amount of allowable amortization per month.

It should be self-evident that you need to keep adequate amortization records of your own. Use the columnar information in Figure 2.1, then add a column (g): *Amortization remaining.* This amount would be column (c) *reduced* by column (f), for each year of activity operation.

Depreciation: Most Understood

In our deferred deductions discourse earlier, we used a second categorical term: *depreciation.* The depreciation concept is quite well understood by most persons in business (as well as by those who are going into business). It applies primarily to tangible property items that are purchased for use in business. Once a new business is up and running, depreciation is more prominent than amortization.

The distinguishing feature of depreciation is the *purchase* of property, in contrast to that which is produced or created in one's business. The idea is that property which is purchased and used — "placed in service" as it is called — will be subject to wear and tear, and exhaustion. It will also be subject to obsolescence as new and better property items come into the marketplace. For this wear and tear, a depreciation deduction is allowed.

Section 167 (**Depreciation**) recognizes the deduction allowance quite straightforwardly. Enacted in 1954, the thrust of Section 167 is expressed in its opening paragraph: subsection (a). The first sentence thereof reads in full as—

There shall be allowed as a depreciation deduction a reasonable allowance for the exhaustion, wear and tear (including a reasonable allowance for obsolescence)—
(1) of property used in the trade or business, or
(2) of property held for the production of income.

This reads clearly enough: "There shall be allowed" . . . a depreciation deduction. But what is a "reasonable allowance"? Interpreting this phrase is where taxpayers and tax agents invariably find themselves at odds. To a taxpayer, the phrase "reasonable allowance" means the maximum deduction possible. To a tax agent, it means the minimum deduction possible.

Over the years, Congress has tried to arbitrate the differing interpretive positions of Section 167, particularly subsection (a). But it has not been very successful. It has tried to clarify the issue of reasonableness by adopting the concept of *class lives*. The attempt was embodied in subsection (m) that read, in part, as:

The term "reasonable allowance" as used in subsection (a) means . . . only an allowance based on the class life prescribed by the [IRS] which reasonably reflects the anticipated useful life of that class of property to the industry or other group.

Under subsection 167(m), now repealed, the IRS formulated 15 class lives, ranging from three to 50 years. Still, the IRS insisted that "reasonable" meant the longest class life possible. The longer the class life, the less the depreciation allowance

Exasperated by the intransigence of the IRS, Congress in 1981 enacted a whole new depreciation section in the tax code. It enacted Section 168: *Accelerated Cost Recovery System*. Evidently, the word "accelerated" was deliberately introduced to counter the IRS's adamant position that "reasonable" always meant the minimum possible depreciation allowance.

Section 168 is a very extensive tax law, which has been amended numerous times since 1981. It is now a complete revision of Section 167.

The "Essence" of Section 168

Section 168 significantly clarifies many of the previous controversies surrounding depreciation. Foremost, it throws out the IRS's intransigent assertion of "salvage value," which meant that an owner could never recover 100% of his cost. It refines the definition of property classes and recovery periods, yet allows some discretion based on business experience and common sense.

All depreciable property used in an active trade or business is now categorized into **eight** recovery classes. These classes set the recovery periods (in years) over which the acquisition cost of the items in each class is 100% recovered. At the end of each recovery class period, if the property is still in service, there is no cost value left. Thereafter, the depreciation deductions cease altogether.

The eight recovery classes are prescribed in Section 168(e): *Classification of Property*. This section reads in part as—

Property shall be classified under the following table:

Class No.	Property shall be treated as:	If such property has a class life (in years) of:
1.	*3-year property*	*4 or less*
2.	*5-year property*	*More than 4 but less than 10*
3.	*7-year property*	*10 or more but less than 16*
4.	*10-year property*	*16 or more but less than 20*

5.	*15-year property*	*20 or more but less than 25*
6.	*20-year property*	*25 or more*
7.	*Residential rental*	*27.5* [straight line]
8.	*Nonresidential realty*	*39* [straight line]

Examples of the kinds of items depreciable in each of Classes 1 through 6 are presented in Figure 2.2. Classes 7 and 8 are rather self-explanatory. They have very long recovery periods (and low rates of depreciation) that may not be of pressing interest to new businesses getting started. It is also doubtful that small businesses would be significantly involved in Classes 5 and 6. Nor would 12-, 25-, and 40-year "alternative depreciation" class lives be appealing.

All property in Classes 1 through 6 must use the *half-year convention* (Sec. 168(d)(1)). This is a presumption that all property placed in service (or disposed of) during the taxable year took place on July 1st of that year. This means that in the first (or last) year of service, the maximum depreciation deduction possible is six months. This is so, even if property is placed in service on January 1st or taken out of service on December 31st. The half-year convention is intended to encourage business owners to place and remove depreciable items more or less uniformly throughout the year, rather than bunching them up into one time frame purely for the tax benefits that may accrue.

To discourage bunching up at year end, a special mid-quarter rule applies: Section 168(d)(3). This rule triggers in when more than 40% of all depreciable items for the year are placed in service during the last three months of the year. When this happens, all property is treated as having been placed in service at the mid-quarter of each calendar quarter in which it is first used. This adds undue complication to your depreciation scheduling. The obvious way out is to avoid placing 40% or more items in service during the months of October, November, and December.

MACRS Depreciation Methods

There is a new buzzword in depreciation circles these days. It is MACRS (M-A-C-R-S). This is an acronym for Modified Accelerated Cost Recovery system. When Section 168 was first enacted in 1981, the acronym then used was ACRS (Accelerated

Cost Recovery System). At that time, ACRS prescribed only four enticingly short recovery periods: 3-, 5-, 10-, and 15-year. In short, MACRS is ACRS made less attractive.

CLASSIFICATION OF PROPERTY : SECTION 168(e)			
Class	Recovery Period	Useful Life	Examples Only [Not all inclusive]
1	3 years	4 or less years	small tools; jigs & dies; computer software; handling devices (baskets, carts, pallets, trays); race horses over 2 years old.
2	5 years	4 to 10 years	autos & light trucks; computers & peripherals (non-main frame); light manufacturing equipment; phones; R&D items; office equipment; medical equipment.
3	7 years	10 to 16 years	furniture & fixtures; heavy-duty vehicles (tractors); storage structures (agricultural, horticultural); large tools & machinery; railroad track; trailers; drilling equipment.
4	10 years	16 to 20 years	railroad tank cars; marine shipping containers; manufactured homes (mobile; theme structures (signs); utility lines & equipment; heavy duty shop machinery; main frame computers; pollution control equipment.
5	15 years	20 to 25 years	production & treatment plants (water, sewerage, steam, gas, electricity, oil); 2-way communication systems; irrigation systems; food processing plants.
6	20 years	over 25 years	locomotives; ships; airplanes; recreational vehicles (pleasure boats); municipal systems (docks, airfields, hangars); roadways, bridges, fences; resource recovery plants; amusement & entertainment facilities (instruments & equipment).

Fig. 2.2 - Example Depreciable items in Each Recovery Period

Whereas ACRS prescribed a separate depreciation method for each of its four recovery classes, MACRS limits the depreciation methods to two (for Classes 1 through 6). These two methods are:

200% declining balance (for Classes 1 through 4)
150% declining balance (for Classes 5 and 6)

The MACRS statutory wording now reads—

Sec. 168(a) — *The depreciation deduction provided by section 167(a)* [pre-1981 law] *for any tangible property shall be determined by using—*

    (1) the applicable depreciation method,
    (2) the applicable recovery period, and
    (3) the applicable convention.

Sec. 168(b) — *The applicable depreciation method is—*

    (1) [For 3-, 5-, 7-, and 10-year property]

        (A) the 200 percent declining balance method,
        (B) switching to the straight line method for the first taxable year for which using the straight line method with respect to the adjusted basis as of the beginning of such year will yield a larger allowance.

    (2) [For 15- and 20-year property]

        (A) the 150 percent declining balance method,
        (B) switching to straight line [as above].

The "switching" to straight line is necessary in order to achieve 100% recovery at the end of each recovery period. Without switching, the declining balance method leaves some unrecovered basis at the end of each period.

Let us illustrate the switching necessity with a numerical example. Consider an item of 5-year property costing $10,000 and placed in service in a new business. The comparative depreciation deductions are as follows:

	200% Declining	Straight line	Switched
1st year (6 mo)	2,000	1,000	2,000
2nd year	3,200	2,000	3,200
3rd year	1,920	2,000	2,000
4th year	1,152	2,000	2,000
5th year	691	2,000	800
Subtotals	8,963	9,000	10,000
6th year (6 mo)	207	1,000	----
Totals	9,170	10,000	10,000

Caution: In order to achieve full recovery in the switched mode, the property must remain in service for the full 12 months of the final year. This means that removal from service (if any) cannot take place until the first month of the following year. (This is the 6th year in the example above.)

Special Election to Expense

Waiting five to six years to tax recover $10,000 in capital costs (as above) does not sit well with entrepreneurs. Businesses, especially new/small businesses, need to recover their capital outlays for depreciable assets as rapidly as possible. Otherwise, much needed capital is tied up for long periods of time. When tied up, the money cannot be used in the business to keep it operating and keep it solvent. Congress was receptive to this concern when it enacted Section 179: *Election to Expense Certain Depreciable Business Assets*.

The idea behind Section 179 is to permit small businesses to get an immediate upfront writeoff (deduction) for selected depreciable expenditures. Here, the term "small business" pertains to the purchase of depreciable items totaling less than $400,000. The maximum upfront deduction is $100,000 (adjusted for price inflation) for each taxable year that Section 179 property is placed in service. "Section 179 property" is defined as *any recovery property* (Section 168) of a tangible nature that is acquired by purchase for 100% use in the active conduct of one's trade or business. We call this: *Full use business property.*

For your familiarization purposes, selected excerpts from Section 179 are as follows:

Subsec. (a) — *A taxpayer* **may elect** *to treat the cost of any section 179 property as an expense which is not chargeable to capital account. Any cost so treated shall be allowed as a deduction for the year in which the property is placed in service* [for "full use" therein].

Subsec. (b) — *The aggregate cost which may be taken into account under subsection (a) for any taxable year shall not exceed $100,000 (beginning after 2002 and before 2008). . . . The amount allowed as a deduction . . . shall not exceed the aggregate amount of taxable income of the taxpayer for such taxable year.*

Subsec. (c) — *An election under this section for any taxable year shall . . . be made on the taxpayer's return . . . in such manner as the* [IRS] *may by regulations prescribe.*

The regulations prescribe that the election to expense (in lieu of depreciation) shall be made in Part I of Form 4562. This portion of the form is subcaptioned: ***Election to Expense Certain Property Under Section 179****. The term "certain property" pertains to all forms of tangible assets (vehicles, machinery, equipment, tools, structures (except real property and its structural components)) used regularly more than 50% of its time in an active trade or business. There are approximately 1,200 words of official instructions that accompany Part I of Form 4562.

Once you have made the Section 179 election, it becomes irrevocable (Sec. 179(c)(2)). That is, you cannot change your mind (without the IRS's consent) after the due date for filing your return. The purpose of this is to prevent you from "playing games" with the depreciation system. Depreciation is an ongoing year-to-year accounting affair. If you purchased 5-year property, for example, and used it for only one year (by selling it or converting it to personal use), there are four years of unused depreciation. You must recapture this unused depreciation equivalence as ordinary income.

Introduction to Form 4562

The official heading on Form 4562 is *Depreciation and Amortization*. It consists of six parts, namely: Part I (Sec. 179 Election), Part II (Prior-year MACRS and Other Depreciation), Part III (Current-year MACRS Depreciation), Part IV (Summary), Part V (Listed Property), and Part VI (Amortization). Parts I through IV appear on page 1; Parts V and VI appear on page 2 (the reverse side of page 1).

The general format and content of Form 4562 (pages 1 and 2) are presented in Figure 2.3. We have edited this form quite extensively, to help you get a better sense of its purpose. It is primarily a current-year summary form. Deductions for prior-year property and expenditures must be scheduled separately on backup records. The depreciation of each property item spans from its in-service date to its out-of-service date.

A headnote on Form 4562 says: *See separate instructions.* These instructions consist of approximately 10,000 words! There is no way that every business taxpayer is going to read every word of these official instructions. Furthermore, the instructions refer you to other IRS forms and publications. Unfortunately, by not reading the official instructions you may wind up underpaying or overpaying your proper tax. All depreciation rules have an impact on the profitability or unprofitability of any new business.

A forewarning to Part I says—

Use Part V for automobiles, certain other vehicles, cellular telephones, certain computers, and property used for entertainment, recreation, or amusement.

Thus, right away, certain items — called "listed property" — are excluded from Part I: Election to Expense (Sec. 179). Listed property has extensive personal/pleasure-use implications. This means that more stringent rules apply for the validation of business use.   After you apply these rules in Part V, you can enter the qualified Section 179 portion in Part I.

Form **4562**	DEPRECIATION & AMORTIZATION	Tax Year

Part I	**Election to Expense Certain Tangible Property**	

- Statutory limit
- Taxable income limit
- Total elective cost
- Carryover of unused

Note: If you have "Listed Property", Complete Part V

Part II	**Other Depreciation: Prior year(s)**

- From Worksheet 4562W
- Pre-MACRS
- Prior MACRS
- Other elections

Do Not Include Listed Property

Part III	**MACRS Depreciation; Current Year**

- 9 property classes
- Alternatives
- 7 columnar entries
- Method/convention

Do Not Include Listed Property

Part IV	**Summary: Enter on "Appropriate Lines" of Return**

- ☐ Listed property (p.2)
- ☐ Nonpersonal items

Part V	**Listed Property - Autos, Phones, Computers, etc.**

Section A: Depreciation Deduction

- 9 columnar entries
- Over 50% BUP

Section B: Information on Use of Vehicles

- ☐ 4 mileage questions
- ☐ 3 other questions
- ☐ Up to 6 vehicles

Section C: Questions for Employers

- 5 questions
- Company cars
- Employee personal uses

Part VI	**Amortization (of Capitalized Expenditures)**

- ☐ Current Amortization
- ☐ Prior Amortization
- ☐ 6 columnar entries
- ☐ Specific code sections

Enter on "Other Deductions/Expenses" Line

Fig. 2.3 - Abridged Format/Contents of Form 4562

We have already discussed the $100,000 election feature of Part I. The only additional point that you need be aware of is that you can exercise the election only for the **more than 50%** business-use portion of listed property in Part V. We'll have more to say on Part V later.

Part II of Form 4562 permits you to use any other-than-MACRS-allowable methods of depreciation that you prefer. The official instructions identify those alternative methods. Included in Part II is MACRS property placed in service in prior years. This means that you have to keep track of such property cumulatively over the years. For this purpose, a separate *Depreciation Worksheet* consisting of 11 columnar entries, is provided in the instructions. The instructions at this point say—

The basis and amounts claimed for depreciation in prior years should be part of your permanent books and records.

Part III of Form 4562 is where most of the nonlisted property action is. It applies only to property placed in service during the *current year.* This portion of the form recapitulates the eight "recovery classes" of MACRS property that we outlined earlier, and adds one other for 25 years. The entry columnar headings are:

(a)   *Classification of property*
(b)   *Month and year placed in service*
(c)   *Basis for depreciation (business-use only)*
(d)   *Recovery period*
(e)   *Convention*
(f)   *Method*
(g)   *Depreciation deduction*

You show all of your MACRS computations directly on Part III. You may also elect, in this part, the 12-year or 40-year alternative depreciation system (ADS).

Part IV of Form 4562 is simply a *Summary* of all depreciation deductions allowed for the taxable year of interest. The line entry instructions there tell you to:

Add the amounts from lines _____ through _____, and enter on the appropriate lines of your return.

Part V: Listed Property

Listed property (autos, computers, cellulars, recreationals, etc.) is a very sensitive tax matter. Computing the proper depreciation allowed takes up most of the space on page 2 of Form 4562. The Part V portion is divided into three sections, namely:

Section A — Depreciation and Other Information
Section B — Information on Use of Vehicles
Section C — Questions for Employers who Provide Vehicles
for Use by their Employees

Part V is devoted exclusively to items that have a high probability of personal use. Its entire thrust is ferreting out the personal use aspects of alleged business uses of property. You must have some documentation on your business use. The ferreting starts right at the beginning of Section A, where you are asked straightforwardly:

Do you have evidence to support the business use claimed?
☐ *Yes*   ☐ *No*
If "Yes," is the evidence written? ☐ *Yes* ☐ *No*

Listed property rules are prescribed in Section 280F. These were enacted in 1984 with the primary focus on expensive (luxury) passenger autos and vans used in business. A "luxury" vehicle is one costing more than $15,000, or more than $25,000 if a truck, van, or electric auto. Other items are luxurious if used in business 50% or less of the time. Much attention in Section 280F is devoted to your establishing the *business use percentage* of items that go on Part V of Form 4562. Business use is in the eyes of the beholder. For this reason, some kind of documentation is needed.

In Section B of Part V, for example, the following questions are asked pertaining to highway vehicles:

1. Total business miles driven   _____
2. Total commuting miles driven   _____
3. Total other (noncommuting) miles driven   _____
4. Total miles driven during the year   _____

5. Was the vehicle available for personal use during off-duty hours? ☐ Yes ☐ No
6. Is another vehicle available for personal use?
☐ Yes ☐ No

The purpose of these and other questions and checkboxes on Part V is to force you to think, document, and write down specific numbers. You must establish quantitatively your true *business use percentage* (BUP). Estimates and guesstimates are simply not acceptable. Your BUP — whatever it turns out to be — has to be expressly entered in a separate column of its own (in Section A). If your BUP is 50% or less, other limitation rules are triggered.

If, as an employer, you allow company-owned vehicles to be used by your employees, you must answer five more questions. The first one is—

Do you maintain a written policy statement that prohibits all personal use of vehicles, including commuting, by your employees? ☐ *Yes* ☐ *No.*

. . . And on and on.

Depreciation Recordkeeping

Except for highway vehicles, Form 4562: ***Depreciation and Amortization*** is used primarily for the year of placement-in-service of business assets. It puts the IRS on notice that you have acquired a productive business asset, have assigned it to an allowable class life, and have documented its acquisition cost. You then compute the amount of acquisition depreciation. Similarly with creation-year data for amortization costs.

We have already informed you that — except for Section 179 items (up to $100,000) — you cannot write off (deduct) your full capital expenditures in the acquisition/creation year. They are recoverable ratably over a statutorily designated number of spread-out years. (Even Sec. 179 property has to be tracked.) How do you keep track of 5-year, 15-year, or 25-year property?

Answer: this is where a Depreciation Recordsheet comes in handy. In its instructions to Form 4562, the IRS provides such a recordsheet. It is titled: ***Depreciation Worksheet (Keep for your records)***. Since no official form number is assigned to this worksheet, we call it Form 4562**W**. Each 4562W can accommodate up to 36 depreciation/amortization schedules. If more space is needed, add continuation sheets.

Each Form 4562W consists of 11 columns whose official headings, preprinted on the form, are—

1. *Description of property*
2. *Date placed in service*
3. *Cost or other basis*
4. *Business use %*
5. *Section 179 deduction*
6. *Depreciation prior years*
7. *Basis for depreciation*
8. *Method/convention*
9. *Recovery period*
10. *Rate or table %*
11. *Depreciation deduction* [current year]

Wherever the word "depreciation" is used in these columnar headings, you can substitute "amortization" when applicable.

There is an unheralded beauty to Form 4562W. If used diligently, you can keep perfect records of your business capital expenditures — and your cost recovery progress — from Day 1 to Day X. Even though its official caption says: *Keep for your records*, we urge, nevertheless, that you attach it to your annual tax return. Doing so signals to the IRS, state agencies, and potential liability litigants that you are loaded for bear. The depreciation/amortization record attaches to any business tax return, whether you become a proprietorship, a partnership, an LLC (Limited Liability Company), an S corporation, or a C corporation.

3

COST OF GOODS SOLD

There Are "Direct Costs" Associated With The Purchasing And/Or Producing Of Goods And Services That Are Sold To Customers. These Costs Become Your First Major Subtraction From Gross Receipts Or Sales. The Two Most Tax-Questioned Items Are Cost Of Labor And Ending Inventory. There Are Two Forms Of Labor: Employees (Form W-2) And Nonemployees (Form 1099-MISC). Be Sure To Carefully Distinguish Between Them. Your Ending Inventory Is "Tied-Up" Capital; It Provides You No Tax Benefits Whatsoever. The Higher Your Ending Inventory, The Higher The Tax On Your Net Profit. Sound Weird?

There is still another branch of capitalization rules (re deferred cost recovery) that you need to know about. As our chapter title indicates, the pertinent rules are called: *Cost of Goods Sold*. In contrast to those deferred recovery rules of Chapter 2 (re amortization and depreciation) that are a below-the-line deduction, your cost of goods sold is an above-the-line deduction. The term "the line" refers to the *Total income* (for the taxable year) of your business venture. An above-the-line deduction is always more tax beneficial than a deduction below the line.

As our chapter title infers — or should infer — there are three tax-accounting concepts involved, namely:

[1] Cost of goods that are produced or purchased in order to be sold.

[2]　Cost of goods actually sold.
[3]　Cost of goods **not** sold, called: *Inventory*

Inventory is something you have to buy, in order to sell something. That "something" requires spending capital for raw materials, semi-finished goods, finished products, parts and supplies, and associated labor. That which is not sold is capitalized . . . and stays on the books. It stays there until the next selling cycle comes around in which all or part of the inventory is sold.

In this chapter, therefore, we want to give you a little insight into the inventory process. We want to explain its features and handicaps in the framework of what the IRS expects of you. To start your awareness in this regard, we have to introduce you to the idea of *gross receipts* and how they include not only receipts from sales, but also receipts from services rendered. Irrespective of the nature of your business, once you start collecting money, there is an income accounting procedure that you must follow. It starts with **Line 1** on your business income tax return.

The Sequence of Income

There are three tax terms that tend to be confusing when operating a business of any size. These terms are (1) Gross Receipts, (2) Gross Profit, and (3) Total Income. They all apply to the *income* portion of your federal returns. They apply whether you are a proprietorship, partnership, LLC, S corporation, or C corporation . . . large or small.

There is no use trying to define each of these terms in words alone. That will only add to the confusion. Instead, we will show the sequence in which they appear. This way, you can compare the terms and sense for yourself why they are chosen for what they are. We will ignore for the time being the actual phraseology used on the official tax forms.

The sequence that we want you to become familiar with is:

1.　**Gross receipts** or sales 　　　　　　　　 _____
　　(derived from customers & clients)
2.　Returns and allowances 　　　　　　　　　 _____
　　(including any sales tax in line 1)

3. Adjusted gross receipts   _____
   (*subtract* line 2 from line 1)
4. Cost of goods sold   _____
   (that go directly to customers & clients)
5. **Gross profit**   _____
   (*subtract* line 4 from line 3)
6. Other income   _____
   (which is not in line 1)
7. **Total income**   _____
   (*add* lines 5 and 6)

This sequence tells you that you arrive at "Gross profit" before you arrive at "Total income." This may not sound right, but it is. Keep in mind that we are concerned with tax accounting: not with ordinary cash flow nor with your anticipation of what to expect for your own take home.

From your gross receipts from customers, you subtract your direct cost of goods and services sold to those customers. This gives you a gross profit figure. (In some cases, this could be a loss instead of a profit.) To your gross profit you add "other income." This is income that is not derived directly from your customers and clients. It represents such monies as various refunds, insurance reimbursements, deposit returns, referral fees, incidental commissions, bank account interest, sales and trade-ins of assets used in the business, and so on.

Your "Total income," therefore, is the sum of your gross profit (or loss) and other business income. It is from this total income that you subtract your administrative and indirect expenses to arrive at your net profit (or loss). We are not going to discuss your net profit (or loss) in this chapter. We want to focus here strictly on the direct cost of goods and services sold to your customers and clients. Even in a service-only business, there'll be direct costs.

The "Direct Cost" Subschedule

One's direct cost in doing business with customers is not a simple, one-line entry item. It consists of several entries — **eight** to be exact. Because all eight direct cost entries are not applicable to every business, a separate subschedule is provided on each federal tax form. The official words used vary slightly depending on the form of business: proprietorship, partnership, LLC, S corporation, or C corporation.

Because this is an instructional guide and not a tax forms preparation guide, we present our edited version of a direct cost subschedule. This we do in Figure 3.1. After reading through the sequence and line items in Figure 3.1, we urge that you mark or flag it in some manner. You want to be able to come back to it easily. We will be referring to it numerous times as we go along.

On Your Federal Income Tax Return			
	Subschedule on Forms 1040, 1065, and 1120		
COST OF GOODS & SERVICES SOLD			
1	Inventory: Beginning of year	1	
2	Purchases for resale	2	
3	Raw materials & supplies	3	
4	Fabrication labor	4	
5	Other direct costs (explain)	5	
6	Subtotal: ADD lines 1 through 5	6	
7	Inventory: End of year	7	
8	SUBTRACT line 7 from line 6 and enter on designated income line	8	↓ ↓ ↓
	COST OF GOODS & SERVICES SOLD ▶		

Fig. 3.1 - Cost of Goods/Services Sold to Customers/Clients

In all cases, the different federal tax forms identify the Figure 3.1 subschedule as: *Cost of Goods Sold.* On Form 1040 (proprietorship), it is identified as Part III, Schedule C; on Form 1065 (partnership), it is identified as Schedule A; and on Form 1120 (corporation), it is also identified as Schedule A. Though functionally a "subschedule," it is a means for summarizing all direct, above-the-line costs for doing business.

The phrase "cost of goods sold" has a direct impact on the profitability of your business. The term "goods sold" is certainly quite clear. It means those goods (and services) **sold to your customers**. This obviously includes purchases for resale, but not those purchases used in-house in the business (such as tools, fixtures, machinery, equipment). Yet, the word "cost" implies all costs — including purchases used in-house — associated with goods sold. This is just not the case.

We think the complete phrase: "Cost of goods and services sold to customers and clients" would be more descriptive of your direct costs. But this is too long. So, we have shortened it to "Cost of Goods & Services." As long as you understand that it means *sold to your customers*, there should be no problem.

Those items of cost which do not go directly to your customers are your "indirect costs." We'll go into your indirect costs (and administrative expenses) in later chapters. Right now, all we want you to be thinking of is—

Direct costs . . . of goods and services
. . . sold to customers (and clients).

This is what Figure 3.1 is intended to detail. Let us discuss each of those line entries separately.

Beginning/Ending Inventories

Lines 1 and 7 of Figure 3.1 use the term "Inventory." Line 1 is beginning inventory; line 7 is ending inventory. The "beginning" refers to the beginning of the tax year; "ending," of course, refers to the end of the tax year. The term "inventory" means merchandise intended for customers on hand at the beginning/ending of each tax year. It includes purchases for resale, finished and partly finished goods, raw materials, and fabrication/shipping supplies that become part of the merchandise you intend to sell.

Between the beginning and ending inventories of a given year, there will be a number of "adjustments" (additions and sub-tractions). Among these are new purchases, newly finished goods, new contract services, mark-ups for price increases by your suppliers, mark-downs for long-held inventory on hand, and write-offs for merchandise destroyed or stolen. You may want to discontinue a certain line of goods and auction it off. If any of your inventory is obsolete or damaged, you may want to junk it or give it away. Whatever you do, record your adjustments in a methodical and systematic way. Do this as you go along; do not wait until the end of the year to record your adjustments.

Preferably make your adjustments during the slow periods of your business year. Adjustments made exactly on your beginning/ending inventory days give the impression that you are "fudging." As a consequence, all last-minute beginning/ending inventory changes are tax suspect.

Your ending inventory of one year becomes the beginning inventory of the following year. These two figures should match exactly. Consequently, for tax purposes, you need "take" only one inventory, namely: that at year end. The ending dollar figure that you show should be documented either by actual physical count or by other sales tracking means.

Purchases for Resale

Good inventory accounting starts with good recordkeeping when you purchase merchandise for resale. When you make such purchases — at least the first time — you have to provide a resale certificate to each of your suppliers. A resale certificate is your rendition of a *Seller's Permit* issued to you by a state's (not federal) sales and use tax collection agency. It enables you to avoid the payment of state sales tax on those resale items that you do not consume in the business itself.

Meanwhile, prudence and care are required in your purchasing procedures. This is because only your purchases for resale (line 2 in Figure 3.1) contribute to your direct costs. In any business, you'll be making other purchases besides those for resale. You must segregate all other purchases from those for resale. This can pose a problem — if you let it — when you purchase resale and nonresale items from the same supplier(s). If you make mixed purchases, we strongly suggest you issue **two** purchase orders: one for resale items and one for nonresale items. If you start in the habit of doing things right, you can avoid many tax-accounting problems down the line. As owner/manager of a business, you will be confronted with these problems . . . sooner or later.

Take additional steps to insure that none of your "purchases for resale" are indeed consumed by you and your family, or are used in your business by yourself and your employees. Food, clothing, and hardware items are commonly used this way. Good self-discipline is required to sort these *personal use* items out, and adjust (downward) your purchases accordingly. You must make this adjustment before making your year-total entry on line 2.

There are several other potential adjustments to your purchases for resale. There are trade discounts, cash discounts, returns and allowances, and price adjustments. A "trade discount" is the difference between the supplier's list price of an article and the actual price that you pay. Many suppliers offer a "cash discount" if you pay within five to ten days or so. If you have to return any merchandise, for whatever reason, you'll be given a refund or allowed a credit in some form. Between the time of your purchase and your resale, there could be price adjustments by your supplier(s). All of these adjustments, plus others as appropriate, have to be made to your resale purchases to truly reflect your costs.

Our suggestion is that you make purchase adjustments directly on the respective purchase invoices to which they apply. Then on each invoice (in a color of your choice) highlight your net purchase cost. Try to keep the invoices in sequential order. This will make it easier for you to summarize your total true *purchase-for-resale* costs for the year.

Raw Materials & Supplies

Purchases for resale imply the acquisition of finished or semi-finished goods. There is another category of purchases for resale called "raw materials and supplies." These purchases consist of parts, materials, chemicals, containers, and other miscellaneous items needed for fabricating and finishing products for sale. These are another segment of costs that go into one's inventory of goods offered for sale to the general public.

Because of the unfinished nature of raw materials and supplies, these items are not as subject to personal use sidetrackings as are the purchases for resale above. In businesses where parts and raw materials are used to fabricate finished or semi-finished goods, there are waste, defective parts, and scrap material lying around. Whether you use some of the raw materials for personal purposes or not, the adjustment effect on direct costs is negligible compared to the amount of waste material thrown away.

There can be some confusion, however, over the term "supplies." Taxwise, there are two classes of supplies. There are direct-cost supplies and indirect-cost supplies. The direct supplies are those used in the fabrication, storage, preparation, and shipping of goods to customers. Indirect supplies are such items as office supplies, small tools, cleaning solvents, stationery, and the like. To distinguish between the two classes, *shop* supplies comprise direct costs whereas office supplies are indirect costs. It is the shop supplies that are included on line 3 (of Figure 3.1).

Meaning of "Fabrication Labor"

We have designated line 4 in Figure 3.1 as fabrication labor. On the official tax forms (1040, 1065, and 1120), this line is labeled: **Cost of labor.** This official phrase is misleading. It implies the cost of all labor, direct and indirect: shop and nonshop. We think that fabrication (in shop) labor provides a more correct cost connotation.

Our "fabrication labor" is a collective term. It includes all labor associated with the design, manufacture, fabrication, production, processing, finishing, and installing those goods that are — or are intended to be — sold to customers.

Unfortunately, the word "labor" is a tax trap. When you make an entry in line 4 you had better be on your guard. Small businesses particularly must distinguish between shop and office labor, and between employees and nonemployees.

To the IRS, its agents and computers, the word "labor" means employees. It means persons on your payroll for whom you prepare, annually, those Forms W-2. If you make any entry in line 4, make sure that the persons you pay are indeed your employees. It's so easy for the Big Computer to cross-check and trap you on this one. You must use intelligent caution.

To signal the IRS that you know what you are doing, insert in the white space on line 4 the number of W-2s that you have issued (or will issue). That is, insert the notation "____ *W-2s.*" This tells them that you are not including nonemployees such as outside vendors, independent contractors, or consultants. The nonemployee labor, if any, is reported on line 5: *Other direct costs.* The official caption is simply: **Other costs.**

Incidentally, nonfabrication labor comprises office workers, salespersons, warehousing personnel, drivers, owners, and the like. This is indirect-cost labor that goes elsewhere on your federal income tax returns. Do not put these persons on line 4 of your direct cost-of-goods schedule.

Nonemployee Labor: Forms 1099

We come now to the catchall portion of your direct cost-of-goods schedule. This is line 5 in Figure 3.1: *Other direct costs (explain)* . . . with a hand notation or a separate attachment.

Line 5 consists of five subcategories of other costs. These are:

(a) Nonemployee labor
(b) Outside fabricators
(c) Installation permits
(d) Freight-in, freight-out
(e) Other miscellany

Let us devote a few paragraphs to nonemployee labor matters. In small businesses, there is widespread temptation to use nonemployees in order to save paperwork and overhead. We encourage you to do so . . . but with your tax eyes open.

Direct cost nonemployees are those who perform fabrication work, consulting services, specialist tasks, and independent contracting. These are part-time, free-lance workers who are not on your regular payroll. Yet, their personal labor is essential for the goods and services that you provide to customers. Some of these persons are in business for themselves; some are employed elsewhere and are "moonlighting" with you; some are part-time workers needing fill-in work; some are unemployed and will accept any job in the hope of becoming employed; and some may be family members and friends for whom you are "doing a favor." You engage most of these persons for specific job assignments of a temporary and non-ongoing nature. You have a business to run; you cannot be paternalistic to everybody. The IRS bureaucracy and its revenue agents do not always understand this.

The IRS can be quite ruthless in trying to assert that all nonemployees are indeed your employees. We will emphasize this matter again in Chapter 4 coming up. We are tipping you off now so that you'll be on guard.

If you engage nonemployees, there are three things you must do, to deflect IRS attacks:

One. You must have each nonemployee read and sign a preprinted *Nonemployee Agreement.* This puts that person on notice that he or she is responsible for his/her own income tax and social security tax matters. The agreement also prescribes other understandings. See Figure 3.2 for an outline of points to be included in such an agreement. Have some paralegal service prepare the agreement for you.

Two. You must insist that each nonemployee submit to you a *Billing Invoice.* Each invoice should contain a brief description of the work performed, the amount charged, and a due date for payment. The invoice(s) should be submitted on a nonperiodic basis, as different phases of the work are completed. If a nonemployee does not have his own preprinted invoices, direct him to an office supply or stationery store where he can purchase a pad of blank invoices to his liking. The nonemployee can write or type thereon the billing information needed.

Three. If you pay a nonemployee the sum of $600 or more in a tax year, you must prepare and submit **Form 1099-MISC.** For this, you need the nonemployee's social security number. A 1099 is comparable, somewhat, to a W-2 — but much simpler. An edited version of Form 1099-MISC is presented in Figure 3.3.

If you engage one nonemployee or more, we have a "must do" for you. You **must** — not *should* — enter in the white space on line 5 (Other direct costs) a notation of the number of 1099s issued. Insert the notation "_____ *1099s.*" Again, you are putting IRS agents on notice that you know what you are doing. You are also indicating that you have the *payer's copy* on hand to back up your entry. You must keep a copy of each issued 1099-MISC form in your records.

Every IRS agent is instructed to request that you produce the payer's copy of every 1099-MISC issued. So, be forewarned!

NONEMPLOYEE AGREEMENT

This **AGREEMENT** is made between

_____ (called "Principal")

and _____ (called "Contractor")

Place of business of Principal: _____

Place of business of Contractor: _____

Work to be performed: _____

End results only. Principal shall exercise no control over Contractor as to manner, means, time, or persons used.

Tools & equipment. Shall be furnished by Contractor at one or more locations as necessary to do the work.

Judgment & discretion. Full right and power of Contractor as he deems necessary to accomplish the work agreed.

Incurrence of liability. Contractor solely liable and responsible for any claims of injury or damage to persons or property.

Available to others. Contractor is free to work for others; however, work above must be completed satisfactorily.

Remuneration by INVOICE. Submission by Contractor of itemized billing for each job or assignment completed.

Responsible for own taxes. Principal shall not withhold income taxes, social security taxes, unemployment taxes, or any other taxes.

Form 1099 - MISC. Will be issued by Principal upon termination of Agreement or at end of each year, whichever appropriate.

Witnessed By	Executed at _____ on _____
_____	_____ /s/ _____ CONTRACTOR Soc. Sec. No. _____
_____	
_____	_____ /s/ _____ PRINCIPAL Fed. I.D. No. _____

Fig. 3.2 - Essential Points in a Nonemployee Agreement

PAYER	1.	FORM 1099 - MISC
	2.	Statement for recipients of
Name & Address		MISCELLANEOUS
	3.	INCOME

Payer's Fed. ID No.	Payee's Soc. Sec. No.	4.

PAYEE	5.	6.
	7. Nonemployee Compensation	8.
Name & Address		
	9. to 13. (see official form)	

Copy A: for IRS	Copy 2: for State	Copy B: for Payee	Copy C: for Payer

Fig. 3.3 - Edited Version of Form 1099 for Nonemployees

Other items listed above that go on line 5 are self-explanatory (more or less). If your line 5 entry consists of more than one category of costs (we listed five categories above), it is a good idea to prepare a separate itemized statement. This is what we mean by the word "explain" at line 5 in Figure 3.1.

Line 6 is the subtotal of lines 1 through 5. There's not much explaining to do here.

Importance of Ending Inventory

It is the ending inventory, line 7, that produces the most dramatic effect on your tax status. The higher your ending inventory, the higher your taxes. The lower your ending inventory, the lower your taxes. Sounds weird, doesn't it?

Let us explain. But, first, turn back to Figure 3.1 on page 3-4.

For a given subtotal of direct costs (line 6), the higher your ending inventory, the lower your cost of goods and services sold (line 8). For a given amount of gross receipts from your customers, the lower your cost of goods and services, the higher your gross profit. The higher your gross profit — all other expenditures being equal — the higher your tax. It's that simple.

By "juggling" one's ending inventory, one's tax burden can be altered to one's taste. We know this; the IRS knows this; and you probably know this. You can count on the fact that your ending inventory could be — will be — the most tax challenged entry of your direct cost items. It is important, therefore, that you take your ending inventory seriously.

There are eight methods for valuing your ending inventory. Of this number, two are commonly used by small businesses. Method A is the *specific cost method*. You simply value your inventory at the end of the year for what you paid for it.

Method B is the "best estimate" method. It consists of checking the inventory on hand either by actual examination or by mental recall, then applying an entrepreneurial "feel" for what it is worth. Method B is not officially sanctioned. Nevertheless, it is frequently used by small businesses. Its weakness is poor documentation for supporting an entry at line 7: ending inventory.

There is a Method 3 called: *Lower of cost or market value* that is officially approved. To use Method 3, you first have to group and classify all like-kind items. Then, *for each grouping*, you have to document your unit costs and — simultaneously — obtain comparable market value information from "third party" sources. You tabulate all of this information and select the lower figure for each grouping. A highly oversimplified example is as follows:

Item	Cost	Market	Whichever is lower
R	$300	$500	$300
S	200	100	100
T	450	200	200
	$950	$800	$600

Short of an actual physical inventory, one popular method is called: *Perpetual book accounting.* This requires continuous (daily) recordkeeping on all purchases/productions **and** on all sales at cost. This method uses ordinary "credits minus debits" accounting practices. It is convenient and practical with appropriate computer software.

The longer you are in business, the more your ending inventory tends to build up. Old merchandise stays around; exchange merchandise is taken in; new merchandise is bought or produced aggressively with the expectation of expanding the business. The result is that your ending inventory grows and becomes a drag on your cash flow and profit picture. This all tends to happen silently . . . and quite unexpectedly.

All ending inventory is tied-up capital. So long as the inventory is on hand, you get no tax benefits for it whatsoever. Even though you may have paid full cash, you get no deduction until it is sold or otherwise disposed. The higher the ending inventory, the higher your bottom-line taxes on income. This exacerbates your desire for, and temptation to, mark down and revalue that inventory.

Vital Role of COG Accounting

The letters "COG" stand for: *Cost of Goods.* It is not always self-evident to new business owners how the COG (as in: *cogwheel*) fits into the scheme of things . . . "above the line." The best way of giving you a quick handle on what we are getting at is our presentation in Figure 3.4. The COG role is clearly displayed there between Adjusted gross receipts and Gross profit. Two COG questions play a major impact on ending inventory data.

One such question asks—

Do the rules of Section 263A (for property produced or acquired for resale) apply? ☐ *Yes* ☐ *No*

Section 263A is captioned: **Capitalization and Inclusion in Inventory Costs of Certain Expenses**. This is a monstrous tax law: over 300 pages of text and regulations! It is designed to force-include most indirect expenses (of producing and reselling) into an intentionally enhanced ending inventory figure. Fortunately, there are two small-business exceptions. There is a "small producer" exception of $200,000; there is a "small reseller" exemption of $10,000,000. If these exceptions apply, be sure to check "No" to the Section 263A question.

The other COG-relevant inventory question is—

Was there any change in determining quantities, costs, or valuations between opening and closing inventory?
☐ *Yes* ☐ *No. If "Yes" attach explanation.*

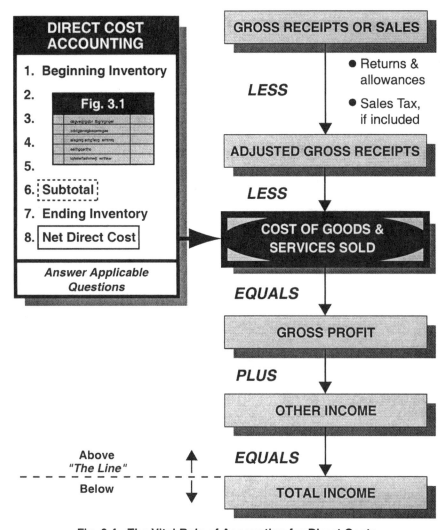

Fig. 3.4 - The Vital Role of Accounting for Direct Costs

If you did change your method, your explanation had better be persuasive. Otherwise, the presumption is that you made the change for tax doctoring reasons. Then the meanness of the IRS comes forth. Let us illustrate what we mean. Suppose that all direct costs for goods and services for the year amount to $365,000. Your corresponding adjusted gross receipts (in Figure 3.4) amount to $500,000. You have no other income. You have two ending inventory values: Case A - "low" at $100,000 and Case B - "high" at $265,000. What is the relative tax consequence of Case A versus Case B?

For Case A, your COG sold amount would be $365,000 – $100,000, or $265,000. Your gross profit would be $500,000 – $265,000, or $235,000.

For Case B, your COG sold amount would be $365,000 – $265,000, or $100,000. Your corresponding gross profit would be $500,000 – $100,000, or $400,000.

For Case A (low ending inventory), you have a low (relatively speaking) gross profit. For Case B (high ending inventory), you have a high gross profit, relative to Case A. Common sense tells you that the tax on a low gross profit ($235,000 for Case A) would be lower than the tax on a high gross profit ($400,000 in Case B). This assumes that all other costs and expenses are unaffected.

But common sense does not tell you about the phenomenon that we've just exposed. Low ending inventory translates into lower taxes; high ending inventory translates into higher taxes.

The moral here is: When starting a new business, do not go overboard with inventory acquisitions. That which is not sold by the end of the year will cost you higher income taxes. Sounds weird . . . but true.

4

EMPLOYEE WITHHOLDINGS

One Publication You "Must Have" Is IRS CIRCULAR E (Employer's Tax Guide). It Gives Tables And Instructions For Income Tax And Social Security/ Medicare Tax Withholdings. Every Employee Increases Your Paperwork For Such Items As Form SS-5 (Social Security Number), Form W-4 (Withholding Allowances), Form 940 (Unemployment Tax), Form 941 (Quarterly Returns), Form 8109 (Tax Deposits) And, Of Course, Form W-2 (Wage and Tax Statement). A Separate File And Separate Payroll Ledger On Each Employee's Wages, Reported Tips, Fringe Benefits, And Expense Allowances Are Required.

There is another tax-related business aggravation that you have to face when starting a business. It relates to engaging employees. It also relates to your withholding of income taxes, social security taxes, medicare taxes, and state unemployment taxes from your employees and "paying over" these withholdings.

If you hire one employee, 10 employees, 100, or 1,000 employees, your tax paperwork is the same. Instead of concentrating on trying to make your business prosper, you are forced into being an unpaid tax collector. You have to withhold money from your employees, add some of your own, and turn it over to federal and state agencies. This is truly an imposition.

There are only two ways to avoid this imposition. One way is to be totally self-employed and have no employees at all. The second way is to engage only independent contractors. Neither of these two alternatives is practical, if you want your business to sustain gross sales in excess of $100,000 while reaching for $1,000,000 or more. So, at some point, you will have to face the tax reality of having employees.

There is irony in your predicament. Not only do you have to impose the government's will on your employees— and fence their complaints — you are actually taxed for the privilege of employing them. This is the "employer tax" aspect of doing business. The taxes on you as an employer are: (a) one-half of the social security tax, (b) one-half of the medicare tax, (c) all of the federal unemployment tax, and (d) all of the state unemployment tax. Also in the works are new federal mandates. Thus, when you hire employees, you are taxed on the possibility of their becoming sick or unemployed and for the day when they retire. These employer taxes are irrespective of any retirement plans and fringe benefits that you might otherwise adopt for your employees.

In this chapter, therefore, we want to explain some of the ramifications you face with respect to withholdings and employer taxation. We have to tell you that you have more responsibilities than privileges, when engaging employees.   Nevertheless, you cannot always avoid employees.

IRS Circular E

When your application for a Federal employer ID number is processed (we'll explain in Chapter 6), you are added automatically to the IRS's Employer Notification Program. That is, unless you instruct it otherwise, it will send you applicable publications, posters, instructions, directives, tax forms, and on and on. Among the mailings is IRS Circular E: **Employer's Tax Guide**. If you do not receive one within 30 days after being assigned an Employer Identification Number (EIN), we urge you to phone the IRS and obtain one. Call the listed number that says: "Tax Forms Only." Circular E is a tax form. We suppose the "E" is for employer/employee.

Circular E consists of 60+ pages of 2-columnar text and tables. On the first inside page, it gives you a tax calendar and due date for completing all of the employer-employee forms you have to file. You are told explicitly that—

This guide tells you about your tax responsibilities as an employer. It explains the requirements for withholding, depositing, reporting, and paying taxes. It explains the forms you must give your employees, those your employees must give you, and those you must send to the IRS and SSA [Social Security Administration]. . . . This guide also has tax tables you need to figure the taxes to withhold for each employee.

Circular E also tells you who your employees are. This is a broad directive which says that—

Anyone who performs services is an employee if you, as an employer, can control what will be done and how it will be done. This is so even when you give the employee freedom of action. What matters is that you have the legal right to control the method and result of the services. . . . The employer usually gives the worker the tools and place to work and has the right to fire the worker.

Circular E is updated every year in January. Every employer should have the latest Circular E in his reference library on tax matters. This is a "must."

In a manner similar to the IRS, state employment-tax agencies also issue their versions of Employer's Tax Guide and Withholding Tables. These state agencies have their own tax calendar and tax forms that you must complete. Thus, not only do you have responsibility to Big IRS, you have responsibility to Little IRS as well.

What If Nonemployees?

As you might suspect, Circular E does not tell you how to qualify some persons as nonemployees. If you had nonemployees, you would escape the withholding and tax reporting responsibilities. Circular E tries to discourage you from even thinking in these terms. In a taunting manner, Circular E says—

If an employer-employee relationship exists, it does not matter what it is called. The employee may be called a partner, agent, or independent contractor. It also does not matter how payments are measured or paid, what they are called, or whether the employee works full- or part-time.

The Circular does go on to say that—

If you have good reason for treating a worker other than as an employee, you will not be liable for employment taxes on the payments to that worker.

This raises the obvious question: What constitutes "good reason" for treating a worker other than as an employee? Circular E avoids discussing this issue altogether. However, this question is addressed in a separate pronouncement of its own: Information Release No. 87-8. This pronouncement cites 20 — yes, 20 — IRS tests that a person must pass in order to have good reason to believe that he/she is not an employee. We summarize these 20 tests for you in Figure 4.1. As you can see, it is very difficult to claim that a worker is a nonemployee.

The summary in Figure 4.1 was specifically designed to thwart the treatment of certain skilled workers as nonemployees. Engineers, designers, drafters, computer programmers, system analysts, and similar persons must be treated as employees if they work at your place of business — or under your direction — on a substantially full-time basis. If you treat these persons as nonemployees, *you* are directly liable for their income tax and social security tax withholdings. If you want a decision as to whether a worker is an employee or nonemployee, file **Form SS-8** with the IRS. Don't expect a decision in your favor.

In other parts of Circular E, the IRS has imposed its will on traditional nonemployees. This includes route salesmen, insurance agents, traveling salesmen, and homeworkers using employer-provided materials and instructions. Even though for income tax purposes these persons may be treated as nonemployees, for social security tax purposes they must be treated as employees. This means that you have to withhold their portion of the social security tax and contribute an equal portion from funds generated by your business. One way around this is to require that each "contractor" be licensed as an independent business.

FACTORS INDICATIVE OF EMPLOYEE STATUS

1. Instructions
  - as to where, when, & how

2. Training
  - under supervision of others

3. Integration
  - directly into daily operations

4. Personal Services
  - using own skills & talents

5. Hiring & firing
  - subject to: by employer

6. Continuity
  - daily ongoing relationship

7. Hours of work
  - when/where set & fixed

8. Time devoted
  - as substantially full time

9. Work on premises
  - not permitted elsewhere

10. Sequences set
  - nil deviations allowed

11. Reports required
  - either oral or written

12. Paid regularly
  - by hour, week, or month

13. Reimbursement
  - for business & travel expense

14. Tools & materials
  - primarily by employer

FACTORS INDICATIVE OF NONEMPLOYEE STATUS

15. Significant investment
  - in facilities (such as office and/or shop) and in major equipment

16. Realization of profit or loss
  - accepting the risks of work performed in a competitive environment

17. More than one customer
  - services for a multiple of unrelated persons or firms at the same time

18. Available to general public
  - continuous offering of services without expectation of long-term hire

19. "Contract" services
  - written or oral, where results are specified, not manner of performance

20. Incurring of liability
  - if results are unsatisfactory, subject to lawsuit & rework

Fig. 4.1 - Factors for Determining Employee/Nonemployee Status

When Hiring Any Employee

Certain tax information must be obtained from every employee when first hired, and supplying it should be a condition of his or her employment. The two most important items in this regard are social security number and Form W-4 (withholding allowances). As simple as it may sound, it is surprising the number of small businesses that hire employees without first getting this information nailed down.

Consider, for example, the social security number. Some potential hirees can't remember their number or they transpose the digits. There are nine digits in that number. The whole world of taxation and tax reporting is keyed to this number. If it is ever incorrectly reported on a tax form, it takes months and years to straighten the matter out. Allow no hiree, therefore, to say that he will provide it to you "later." You want it now, or no hire-on.

As an employer, your best protection is to insist on seeing the hiree's **Social Security Number Card**. This is that wallet-size little card issued by the Social Security Administration (SSA). This card displays the social security number in bold red figures, followed by the typed full name of the person and his/her handwritten signature. We strongly urge you to *photocopy* this card. Then attach the photocopy to the record on that employee.

If a hiree does not have a social security card, insist that he obtain one. It is not your concern why he does not have one; it is your concern that he have one. For this purpose, instruct the hiree to fill out **Form SS-5**: *Application for a Social Security Card* (Original, Replacement, or Correction). It is a good idea for you to have a stack of SS-5 forms (and instructions) on hand at all times. Get them from the IRS or SSA. You also should know the address of the nearest Social Security office to your place of business. Even prepare a little map with directions and the SSA phone number. A lot of hire-on time can be saved, with accurate knowledge on how to get a social security card.

The next matter, before taking on an employee, is Form W-4. This form is officially titled: *Employee's Withholding Allowance Certificate*. Note that this is *not* an "exemption" certificate; it is a "withholding allowance" certificate. You also should have a stack of these forms on hand at all times.

Before you take any withholding from an employee's pay, you want to have an *originally signed* Form W-4 in your possession. This form provides the employee's full name, current address, and his marital status. If an employee delays in providing you with his W-4, treat him as a single person with one allowance only. Do not try to guess and do your employee a favor. If it turns out later that he has to pay additional income taxes (beyond the withholdings) he is going to blame you. Technically, you should request a new W-4 from each employee at the beginning of each year.

Separate Record on Each Employee

In some businesses, employer-employee tax problems can be irritating. The problems can haunt you up to as much as five years after termination of an employee. In addition, there can be labor and legal problems: disputes over pay, reimbursement for expenses, fringe benefits, and so on. It is important, therefore, that you keep an entirely separate record on each employee. Do not try to shortcut and combine several employee records. You want each record to be an archival stand-alone.

In the record file of each hire-on, you should have an *Employment Agreement.* This should be one or two pages of particulars. It should be read and signed by the hire-on, and should be countersigned by you or a member of your staff. The amount of compensation should be indicated, together with the hours of work expected, some standard of performance, designation of the work place (or sales territory), and the furnishing of tools, vehicles, and incidental materials. A statement of your policy on expense reimbursement, fringe benefits, and retirement plans (if any) should be included. We discourage the setup of pension and profit-sharing plans until you have been in business for at least three years. If you have no such plans, you should state so in the employment agreement. This way, an employee may be eligible to set up his own IRA plan. (IRA = Individual Retirement Account.)

If you have to terminate an employee for any reason, you must prepare for the file a memorandum of the circumstances therewith. Terminated employees may find it necessary to apply for unemployment benefits. Each application for said benefits will be followed by an inquiry to you. On state official forms, you will be asked to verify the termination, the cause, and length of service of the employee. Unless you keep a written record on each employee, you may have to grope and guess.

One of the common problems in a small business is the rapid turnover of employees. Often, they are young persons trying to test their own interests. Because of this turnover, a *probation period* is recommended. To save tax paperwork during the probation, it is advisable to contract with a temporary service agency to supply the workers you need. This way, the temporary service agency becomes the employer who has to keep the tax and other records. A temporary service contract of from three to six months should be adequate to determine whether you want to take on a worker as a regular employee. This will cost you about 20% more than a direct hire-on.

As an indication of the amount of paperwork required on each employee, we present Figure 4.2. Note that the central tax document is a payroll ledger. The intended message in Figure 4.2 is that, when you take on any employee, your tax duties are increased substantially.

Payroll Ledgers & Pay Periods

On the very day that a new employee starts, you should set up a payroll ledger in his or her behalf. Do not wait until the first payday arrives. Formulate the payroll ledger the moment an employee reports aboard. Obtain and record his full name, current address, social security number, marital status, and the W-4 withholding allowances. Each employee will have payroll particulars of his own.

Make sure that each employee understands the "pay period" for payroll purposes. This is the period for which the *base pay* is computed. It may be weekly, biweekly (every two weeks), semimonthly (twice a month), or monthly. Other periods may be used, but these are the most common. Separate tax withholding tables (in Circular E) are based on each of these periods.

In addition to base pay, there may be supplemental pay such as prizes and awards, bonuses, commissions, sick pay, and so on. Included in the "and so on" are taxable fringe benefits. In some businesses, tips become an important element in an employee's gross pay. If an employee receives tips of $20 or more in a month, he is supposed to report the total amount to you. These are known as *taxable tips* that you include on his payroll ledger. In food and beverage establishments, *allocated tips* (also taxable) are assigned to each employee whether he/she reports them to you or not.

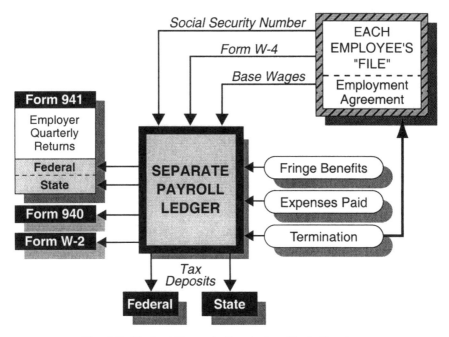

Fig. 4.2 - Typical Records Needed on Each Employee

A *gross pay* column should be highlighted (on the ledger) to tally all of the separate forms of compensation due each employee. This includes the taxable fringes and taxable tips. It is to the gross pay that the income tax withholdings apply. There are federal income tax withholdings and state/local income tax withholdings (where applicable).

Altogether, there are from four to six separate *required withholdings* from the compensation due each employee. The variation depends on state and local tax laws, and on whether any taxable tips are reported to you. The required withholdings are—

1. Federal income tax (FIT)
2. Social security tax (SST)
3. Medicare tax (MCT)
4. State income tax (SIT)
   (except for those states which have no income tax)
5. State disability insurance (SDI)
6. Local income tax (LIT)

(for those few cities, regions, and counties that require it)

In addition to the required withholdings, there may be voluntary withholdings. These could be savings plans, group health payments, and loan repayments. There may also be involuntary withholdings. There could be court-ordered child and/or spousal support payments, tax liens for prior delinquencies, and other judgment liens. As an employer, you are responsible for these withholdings also.

Employer Quarterly Returns

Regardless of your chosen form of business startup, make sure that your payroll ledgers and/or computer software are formatted into four calendar quarters for the year. The reason is that, if you have one employee and withhold so much as $1 from that employee, you become locked in to a quarterly tax reporting system. In the federal domain you are required to file Form 941: *Employer's Quarterly Federal Tax Return.* Similarly, states also have their version of quarterly employer returns.

The term "quarterly" means every three months . . . without fail. These calendar quarters are as follows:

Quarter	Ending	Due Date
Jan – Feb - Mar	Mar. 31	Apr. 30
Apr – May – Jun	Jun. 30	Jul. 31
Jul – Aug – Sep	Sep. 30	Oct. 31
Oct – Nov – Dec	Dec. 31	Jan. 31

As you can see, the due date of these returns is 30 days after the end of each quarter. For each whole or part month that a return is filed late, there is a 5% penalty. The penalty is paid by the employer: *not* by the employees. This is what we mean by being "locked in" to the system.

To introduce you to Form 941, we present a much simplified and highly edited version of it in Figure 4.3. We have generalized the form so that you will understand its purpose, without bogging you down with preparatory details. Whether you complete the form yourself, or have a payroll service agency do it for you, is another matter. However prepared, you would be the one to sign it. As the business owner, therefore, you should be fully aware of all employee tax matters.

Form 941	EMPLOYER'S QUARTERLY FEDERAL TAX RETURN		
Name (of owner) _____ Trade Name _____ Address _____ _____	Quarter Ending	☐ Mar 31 ☐ Jun 30 ☐ Sep 30 ☐ Dec 31	
	Employer I.D.No. _____		
1	Total wages, tips, & other compensation		
2	Total income tax withheld		
3	Adjustments (if any): Explain		
4	Adjusted total income tax withheld		
5	Social security wages & tips	x 12.4%	
6	Medicare wages & tips	x 2.9%	
7	Adjustments (if any): Explain		
8	Adjusted total social security & medicare tax		
9	Total taxes (add lines 4 & 8)		
10	Total deposits for quarter		
///	BALANCE DUE (subtract line 10 from line 9)		
///	(If less than $2,500) PAY TO IRS		
RECORD OF MONTHLY DEPOSITS *If line 9 is $2,500 or more.*			
Date(s) Wages Paid	1st Month	2nd Month	3rd Month
Total deposits for quarter. Enter at line 10 ▶ [ ]			
___ Signature	___ Title	___ Date	

Fig. 4.3 - Simplified Version of Quarterly Form 941

In Figure 4.3, we have emphasized certain key lines that you should know about. The first line of importance is "Wages, tips, and other compensation" paid during the quarter (line 1). This is the gross amount against which employee income taxes are withheld. These withholdings appear on lines 2 through 4 (in Fig.

4.3). These withholdings are *not* your money. Other than your time and effort, you contribute nothing towards these withholdings. They are 100% employees' money.

Lines 5 through 8 (in Fig. 4.3) are social security and medicare tax matters. The spaces are for entering the amount of wages, tips, and other compensation to which the social security and medicare taxes apply. In some cases, this is not the same as the amount on line 1. This is because certain kinds of employees and certain kinds of payments are not subject to the social security/medicare tax. To determine whether or not a certain amount is exempt from social security/medicare tax, we refer you to Circular E. Look for the table headed: *Special Classes of Employment and Special Types of Payment.* Then look down the column headed: "Social Security and Medicare." There are approximately 75 entries in that table: far too many for us to discuss here.

Whatever the amount of taxable social security/medicare compensation there may be, the employee contributes 50% of the tax. You, as the employer, also contribute 50% of the tax. For this reason, you must take particular care to note the amount on line 8 in Figure 4.3. On the official Form 941, it is a different line number. This is because there are seven permitted adjustments you could make. Whatever the *Adjusted total* of social security and medicare tax may be, 50% of such amount is deductible by you as a business expense. You have to establish your own records for tracking your 50% "contributions."

FTD "Coupons" Explained

Now that you have withheld and collected money from your employees, and have contributed 50% of their social security/medicare tax, what do you do with this money? Do you forward it to the IRS, quarterly, when you file Form 941?

In most cases, "No."

Only when the amount withheld, or amount due, at the end of any quarter is less than $2,500, can you forward the money directly to the IRS. In all other cases, you must present the money — in cash, check, or money order — to an *authorized depository.* This generally is any commercial bank that is a member of the Federal Reserve System. But you just can't hand the money to them. You must use Form 8109: *Federal Tax Deposit Coupon* (FTD "coupons" for short).

There are special deposit rules that tell you when to use the FTD coupons. For details on these rules, we refer you again to Circular E. In general, if the withholdings are less than $2,500 for the quarter, you deposit monthly. If the withholdings are $12,500 or more, you make deposits weekly.

On each FTD coupon, there are entry boxes for indicating the type of tax and the tax period against which the deposit is to be applied. Take great care to mark the entry boxes properly. Otherwise, the deposit coupons will generate many computer mismatchings from bank to IRS, and from IRS to you. Any additional taxes due, or penalties asserted, fall on your shoulders: not on the "authorized" depository bank.

Even though you make your deposits to the bank on time, the bank may electronically report them late to the IRS. If this happens, there is a late payment penalty of 5% that you must pay. The same 5% penalty applies if you get disgusted with the bank and make your deposits directly with the IRS. Apparently there is some behind-the-scenes arrangement between the IRS and the Federal Reserve banks. You have no depository choice.

Additionally, another depository mandate exists. If the total of all required deposits (income tax withholdings, social security tax, medicare tax, and other employer taxes) exceeds $50,000 in any year, you must make *electronic deposits* for all subsequent years. This is the IRS's much heralded *Electronic Federal Tax Payment System* (EFTPS). Once you are required to make EFTPS deposits, any subsequent failure to do so is subject to a 10% penalty. All depository penalties are frustrating and irritating. You are not notified of them until six to 12 months after each deposit.

Income taxing states also require employer quarterly returns. Included are disability, unemployment, and training taxes. The state filing quarterly dates correspond to the federal dates.

Still Another Form: 940

There is another federal employer form that you need to be aware of. This is Form 940: *Federal Unemployment Tax Return*. It is filed only once a year. It is referred to as the FUTA form.

The FUTA tax is approximately 6% of the first $7,000 in wages paid to each employee during the year. We say "approximately" (6% on $7,000) because these figures change slightly from year to year. The important point is that you — as the employer — have to pay this tax. It is not withheld from the employee's wages. It is a pure tax on you in the event you have to lay off a worker.

In virtually every state, you also have to pay unemployment tax. If you pay into a state unemployment fund timely, and in the proper amount, you are allowed a credit against the FUTA tax. This credit is approximately 5% of the first $7,000 in wages paid. The net effect is that the FUTA tax, after adjustment for state credits, is approximately 1% of the $7,000 wages paid. The end result, however, is that you pay unemployment tax to both state and federal authorities.

If your FUTA tax is more than $100 for the year, it must be deposited quarterly. You have to use the same FTD coupons that you use for depositing withholding taxes and social security taxes. If you have two or more employees for the year, each earning $7,000 or more, your FUTA tax will be over $100. If your undeposited FUTA tax is less than $100 at the end of the year, you may pay it directly to the IRS when filing Form 940.

Taxability of Fringe Benefits

The taxability of, and withholdings from, fringe benefits to employees are punitive aggravations to employers. Even as a small business employer, it is difficult to avoid entirely allowing certain fringe benefits to employees. Sick pay, prizes and awards, discounts on merchandise and services, meals and snacks on premises, use of company car, health plans, educational assistance, and so on, are customary practices by most employers. Some of these benefits are taxable and some are not. The distinction is not crystal clear.

The IRS position is that all fringes are taxable unless specifically designated as nontaxable by law. The rationale is that the fringe benefits are variant forms of compensation that are conferred only on employees. They are not conferred upon ordinary customers and clients of the business. Once a fringe benefit is characterized as taxable, it is subject to income tax withholdings *and* to social security/medicare tax withholdings. The same applies to bonuses and to nonstatutory stock options.

To help clear up the ambiguities, Section 132(a): ***Exclusion from Gross Income*** is particularly relevant. It says—

Gross income shall not include any fringe benefit which qualifies as a—
(1)   no-additional-cost service,
(2)   qualified employee discount,
(3)   working condition fringe,
(4)   de minimis fringe,
(5)   qualified transportation fringe,
(6)   qualified moving expense reimbursement, or
(7)   qualified retirement planning services.

Other portions of Section 132 define these terms, and the limitations with respect to spouses, children, and parents of employees. Also included are treatment of certain eating facilities, qualified employee discounts, and parking on business premises.

The essence of Section 132: ***Certain Fringe Benefits*** is that the benefits conferred must be essential to doing business. They must be necessary for carrying on the business, as opposed to some additional bonus to employees. For example, meals, snacks, and beverages furnished at the employer's place of business during public business hours are construed as "for convenience of the employer." In other words, by providing these items on premises, there is no disruption in the flow of business. Similarly for employee discounts on merchandise and services. So long as the discounts do not exceed profit markups or are comparable to those offered to the public for promotions and special sales, they are nontaxable to employees who receive them.

Group health plans instituted under Section 106(a) are not taxable, provided there are no discriminatory benefits to "highly compensated" employees. Compensation for personal injuries or sickness are not taxable, provided the conditions in Section 104(a) are strictly met. There are exceptions for excess compensation over those amounts actually incurred for medical, dental, and pharmaceutical services. The nontaxable provisions apply to workmen's compensation (under state law), injury awards in lawsuits, and insurance payments for accidents and illness.

Except for the above, virtually every other fringe benefit is taxable (IRS Reg. 1.61-21). For example, "sick pay" — which is the continuation of one's wages while sick — is fully taxable, if paid by the employer out of his business proceeds. The personal use of a company car (for commuting, for week-ends, or for vacations) is also fully taxable. The same applies to the use of any company facilities for personal lodging, transportation, entertainment, or recreation. The tax problem is determining the "fair market value" of these benefits for inclusion in each employee's gross pay. If an employer undervalues these benefits, he is subject to an excise tax (another penalty).

The taxability of fringe benefits is an onerous task for small businesses. We suggest, therefore, that you limit your employee benefits strictly to Section 132 working condition fringes and to Section 106 group health plans. Forego all other benefit programs. If the competition forces you to reconsider, offer, instead, a commensurate increase in each employee's base pay.

Business Expense Reimbursements

In some businesses, employees will incur legitimate expenses in furthering the business interests of the employer. The employer tax concern becomes: How should these expenses be reimbursed? Should the employee be given a "standard allowance," such as a car allowance, per diem, travel allowance, entertainment allowance? Or, should he be reimbursed dollar-for-dollar for the actual (substantiated) expenses incurred?

For small businesses, we highly recommend the dollar-for-dollar reimbursement method. Here's why.

Any standard allowance that you provide is fully tax reportable. It is "other compensation" to your employees. This means that it is subject to income tax withholding, and, in many cases, subject to social security tax withholdings also. This reportability and the withholdings are going to make your employees very unhappy. They'll have to justify their business expenses to the IRS, before any deductions (on their tax returns) will be allowed.

Some years ago, the rules for employee business expense deduction were tightened severely. To get any deduction at all, the expenses have to be classified into those that are reimbursed, and those that are not reimbursed. Separate tax forms are required for each. And before any business expense deduction form can be used, the employee must have perfect records. Every penny of expenditure must be positively documented. In practice, the employee business expense rules are inordinately unreasonable.

A far better way to go is the dollar-for-dollar reimbursement method. This, in tax jargon, is the *adequate-accounting-to-employer* rule. This rule says that, where there is adequate expense accounting by the employee to his employer, and the employer reimburses the employee dollar for dollar, there is no taxability to the employee and no tax withholding by the employer. The term "adequate accounting" means that the employee submits a written expense voucher to the employer, with all supporting substantiation attached.

So that you know the dollar-for-dollar method is valid, let us cite the IRS regulatory language. We refer to Regulation 1.274-5A(e)(2)(i): ***Reimbursements equal to expenses***. It reads—

> *For purposes of computing tax liability, an employee need not report on his tax return business expenses for travel, transportation, entertainment, gifts, or with respect to listed property paid or incurred by him solely for the benefit of his employer for which he is required to, and does, make an adequate accounting to his employer and which are charged directly or indirectly to the employer or for which the employee is paid through advances, reimbursements, or otherwise, provided that the total amount of such advances, reimbursements, and charges is equal to such expenses.*

Obviously, there is no point in going through all of the tax hassle if you can set up internal procedures to comply with Regulation 1.274-5A(e)(2)(i). There is a simple way to do this. Prepare your own expense voucher forms, or select among those preprinted forms commercially available. Then instruct your employees to submit their vouchers to you on whatever periodic basis is appropriate for the expenses incurred.

After examining the vouchers for reasonableness and legitimacy, reimburse the employee by check for the exact amount approved. This way, you get a business tax deduction for the expense. Best of all, it is not tax reportable by your employee(s). Such reimbursement is primarily for your benefit, anyhow.

Getting Out Those W-2s

There's one chore each year that you probably already know about. It's getting out those Forms W-2. In case you haven't scrutinized a W-2 lately, its official heading is: *Wage and Tax Statement.* This is the summary form that you must prepare and present to each employee, on or before January 31 of each year.

To alert you to a few key points in preparing a W-2, we present an abbreviated version of the form in Figure 4.4. Note that we purposely have emphasized Boxes 1, 12, and 14.

Box 1 is labeled: *Wages, tips, other compensation.* This box is where you enter the gross annual remuneration to an employee, whether subject to withholdings or not. The amount entered must be the grand total of all cash, check, and noncash payments. This means that Box 1 includes not only what is normally considered wages and tips, but every form of "other compensation." This is where employee confusion will arise.

The term "other compensation" includes all taxable fringe benefits, unvouchered travel reimbursements, car allowances, expense allowances, use of company property and services, excess employee discounts, sick pay, bonuses, prizes, awards, life insurance premiums, and so on. Since these items are not paid regularly throughout the year like wages, most employees tend to forget about them. They are shocked when Box 1 shows an amount greater than their normal wages. They will argue that you overstated the Box 1 amount. They will insist that you provide them promptly with an itemized breakdown.

Fortunately, there are boxes 12 and 14 on Form W-2. In Box 12, you enter the total value of all taxable fringe benefits in Box 1. Box 12 enables you to enter up to four different code symbols from a preprinted choice of 20 (in the instructions for preparing Form W-2). If more than four code symbols are required, you are authorized to prepare a supplemental statement to Box 12. Box 14 is for listing any other information you want to impart to each employee, explaining any oddities on the W-2.

Form W-2	Wage & Tax Statement			Year
EMPLOYER'S ID	**1** Wages, tips, etc. & other compensation		**2** Federal income tax withheld	
EMPLOYER'S Name, address, ZIP	**3** Soc. Sec. Wages		**4** Soc. Sec. tax withheld	
	5 Medicare Wages		**6** Medicare tax withheld	
	7 Soc. Sec. tips		**8** Allocated tips	
EMPLOYEE'S ID	**9** EIC payments		**10** Dependent care	
EMPLOYEE'S Name, address, ZIP	**11** Nonqual plans		**12** Benefit codes	
	13 ☐ ☐ ☐		*see*	
	14 Other		*instructions*	
Copy C - for EMPLOYEE'S RECORDS			*for Box 12*	

15	**16**	**17**	**18**	**19**	**20**
Employer's State ID	State wages, etc.	State income tax	Local wages, etc.	Local income tax	Locality

Fig. 4.4 - Edited/Abbreviated Version of Form W-2 for Employees

It is not our intention to tell you how to prepare the W-2 forms. Ample official instructions are available for this purpose. We do want you to be aware, however, of Boxes 2, 4, and 6. Box 2 is the total federal income tax that you withheld. Box 4 is the total social security tax that you withheld. Box 6 is the total medicare tax that you withheld. You must reconcile these three totals with those quarterly employer returns that you filed throughout the year.

How do you transmit your Forms W-2 to proper authorities? There is only one federal "proper authority," namely: the Social Security Administration (SSA). You send all Copies A there via Form W-3: *Transmittal of Wage and Tax Statements*. A W-3 instruction tells you where to file and to file Form W-3 even if you have only one Form W-2 to transmit.

Altogether, you have to prepare at least six copies of each W-2 for each employee. The official copy sequence is as follows:

Copy A — to Social Security Administration
Copy B — to employee for filing with Federal return
Copy C — to employee for his/her own tax record
Copy D — to be retained by employer (you)
Copy 1 — to State, City, or Local Tax Department
Copy 2 — to employee for filing with Local return(s)

If an employee loses or destroys his set of W-2s (Copies B, C, and 2), you have the choice of redoing a set and marking it "Reissued," or, you can make three photocopies of your Copy D, and re-mark them as Copy B, Copy C, and Copy 2.

If an employee stops working for you before the end of the year, you have 30 days after the termination to furnish him (or her) Copies B, C, and 2. Or, if the employee consents, you can wait until you prepare the W-2s for all of your employees. However, be sure that you have every terminated employee's latest mailing address. Otherwise, you'll be getting frantic phone calls and letters as April 15th approaches.

5

BANK DEPOSITS DISCIPLINE

Those Deposits That You Make At Your Bank(s) Are "Third-Party" Records. As Such, They Are Available For IRS Scrutiny At Any Time. Once Aware Of This, You Will Segregate Your Deposits By Tax Character And You Will Retain The Confirmation Statements. One Day, The IRS Will Want To Compare Your Total Bank Deposits With The Total Positive Income Reported On Your Tax Return(s). All Business Expenditures, Supported With Canceled Checks, Should Be Codified By Category And Indexed To Specific Line Numbers On Your Return(s). For Best Banking Discipline, 3 Principal Accounts Are Urged (Business, Personal, And Investment).

Every new business needs capital (money). We have stressed this in various ways, previously. The problem is that most businesses start woefully undercapitalized. The minimum possible upfront money is advanced personally, with the expectation that the business will "bootstrap" itself on its sales. This seldom happens in an active trade or business.

Buyers do not always pay cash. Some will take 30, 60, or 90 days to pay. The larger the buyer, the longer the delay in payment. In the meantime, you have operating expenses to pay and cost of goods to be financed. If you have employees, they are priority payees whose withholdings are **not** your money. Before long, a vicious cycle of trying to borrow, fending off creditors, and delaying taxes sets in. Matters get out of control. Tax authorities step in. They want their money now, and threaten to either shut the business down or impose penalties that force you to shut down.

Many of the undercapitalization problems can be avoided, we believe, by good bank deposits procedures. Indeed, disciplined bank accounting — which includes controlled access to lines of credit — is *the key* to averting the failure of any new business.

Good banking habits must start right at the beginning of your business. Don't be fooled by all of the electronic wizardry being offered by banks and financial institutions these days. Avoid those grandiose sweep accounts, electronic transfers, all-purpose investment printouts, and the mixing of personal matters with your business banking. "Putting it all on the computer" is not going to relieve you of the down-to-earth self-discipline that you need. When the chips are down, you cannot beat the old-fashioned handwritten (or typewritten) disbursement checks and the handwritten (or typewritten) deposit slips. When you get through reading this chapter, you will understand better why we say this.

Those Records at Your Bank

In case you haven't realized it, we no longer have a true free enterprise system these days. Nor do we have so-called "financial privacy." Once you are in business with a Federal ID Number, the IRS can monitor your banking procedures like a hawk. On short notice, it can demand that you produce the records for them, or it can gain access to your bank information without your consent. In IRS eyes, you are in business solely for the purpose of generating revenue for the U.S. Treasury.

To give you some of the flavor of what we are getting at, several years ago a leading San Francisco newspaper ran the following advertisement—

IRS SPECIAL AGENT

Immediate opportunities exist with the IRS as special agents/ criminal investigators. Duties involve <u>analyzing bank records</u>, executing search warrants, surveillance, making arrests, use of firearms and testifying in trials. [Underscoring supplied.]

Oh, that's for crooks and tax cheats," you say. "They won't look at my bank records. I'm doing nothing wrong. Besides, they don't have the authority to go to my bank without my consent. That's invasion of privacy!"

Well, well.

Be introduced, now, to the following six sections of the Internal Revenue Code:

Sec. 7601 — Canvassing for Taxable Persons and Objects

Sec. 7602 — Examination of Books and Witnesses

Sec. 7603 — Service of Summons

Sec. 7604 — Enforcement of Summons

Sec. 7605 — Time and Place of Examination

Sec. 7606 — Entry of Premises for Examination of Taxable Objects

The term "taxable objects" means . . . *any books, papers, records, or other data that may be relevant or material.* Thus, the combined effect of these six sections is that the IRS can get to your bank records whenever it wants to. In theory, there must be some pretense that tax is due. In practice, a $1 allegation provides sufficient cause. The IRS can go to your bank in the daytime, or at night, if it is open then.

In Section 7609(a): ***Special Procedures for Third-Party Summons***, your bank is defined as a *third-party recordkeeper*. As such, your bank records AT THE BANK belong to the bank: not to you. True, it is your business financial information that goes to the bank. But that's not the point. The records are "third party." This means that the IRS need give your bank only three days' notice. After that, the bank has to produce its records on you, whether you consent or not.

Please do not misunderstand. We're not trying to put the fear of God in you. We just want you to face reality. We don't want you to be blind and blithe about your banking procedures. If you are truly aware that your financial transactions — especially when in business — are an "open book" for the IRS at any time, you'll take prompt action to avoid surprises.

Ordinarily, the IRS will not go to your bank (or other financial institution) on its own whim. Except in rare criminal investigatory cases, it first seeks your bank records from you. A "bank," incidentally, is a *depository* institution through which financial transactions are processed in the normal course of business. Therefore, what the IRS is primarily interested in is the TOTAL DEPOSITS that you made, and how this total reconciles with the income reported on your business tax returns.

A Nightmarish Example

Not long ago, a small business owner (let's call him Big Foot Instrument Co.) received a "routine" form letter from the IRS. In those parts pertinent to our discussion, it read—

Your return for the above year has been selected for examination. Please provide the following:
- *All records and books to determine income (deposit slips, check registers, cash receipts, sales journals, books of account, account numbers, . . . and any other records used to determine income).*
- *All records, contracts, statements, and any other documentation of nontaxable income.*
- *Monthly statements for all financial accounts, both business and personal.*

If you were to receive a similar IRS demand, what would *you* do? Could you pull together in one place "all records of income"?

The gross sales and other income from the Big Foot business totaled $294,000 . . . as reported on his tax return.

In the case at hand, there were five different financial accounts. All were handled by the same bank. The types of accounts and the total deposits in each (for the year at issue) were:

1. The business account $224,000
2. Line-of-credit account   115,000
3. Personal checking account   327,000

4.	Rental collection account	32,000
5.	Personal investment account	138,000
	Grand total deposits	$836,000

Big Foot reported $294,000 on his tax return. What accounts for the difference of $542,000 (836,000 minus 294,000)? Is it income not reported? If so, it is fully taxable . . . plus penalties . . . plus interest.

Now you must surely feel the anguish and nightmares that owner Big Foot went through. To make matters worse, he destroyed all of his deposit slips and his investment redemption statements. He did "everything by computer." He engaged profusely in telephone transfers between accounts. His line-of-credit was automatically re-extended when his loan balance was paid down below $100,000. Since all of his accounts were with the same bank, all monthly statements looked alike, except for the 15-digit account numbers.

In Big Foot's own heart, he knew that all of his taxable income was properly reported. But how would he prove this to a skeptical government agent whose grand promotion is riding on the additional revenue from a $542,000 "discrepancy"?

This is a perfect example of what careless banking habits can do. It's all so easy with a telephone and a computer. The IRS simply will not accept your computer printouts and/or e-files. Thus, until you have been through the bank-deposits-analysis-wringer by a tax agent drooling for more revenue, you cannot imagine the pain and suffering that lie in wait. If your business grosses more than $100,000, then you, too, are vulnerable.

How It All Worked Out

In the example above, the $32,000 rental collection account was not Big Foot's own money. A close business friend who owned several apartment complexes went on a foreign vacation for three months. He asked Big Foot to be his collection agent while he was gone. Of course, there was no contract; no written agreement; just a verbal understanding. To keep the rent money separate, Big Foot opened a separate account in his own name, with his own bank. Most of the money was used to pay operating expenses. When the friend returned, the balance in the rental account was turned over to him. It took a long, hard time to prove this to the tax agent. It was not until the agent examined the friend's bank account that he allowed the $32,000 as an offset against Big Foot's $542,000 discrepancy. The reduced discrepancy now stood at $510,000.

Next came the $115,000 line-of-credit account. These were not actual deposits but were repayments on a cumulative $215,000 loan that the bank had advanced to Big Foot. The repayments came from Big Foot's other three accounts (business, personal, and investment). But every repayment (about 15 in all) had to be individually traced. This necessitated showing 15 origins in the three accounts and tracing each one through e-transfer by e-transfer. In the process, approximately 56 monthly statements had to be sorted through and studied. In agonizing time, Big Foot prevailed. The tax agent allowed a $115,000 offset against the $510,000 discrepancy. The revised discrepancy now stood at $395,000 — still a long substantiation way to go.

The next matter was: Where did the $215,000 line-of-credit loans go? Big Foot contacted his bank to help him establish the amount and date that each loan originated. He repeatedly asked for a computer printout summary. The bank fouled this up miserably due to its interoffice retrieval problems and due to the fact that the bank's central loan office was some 1,500 miles away. Finally, though, he got the summary showing that eight loans were advanced to him. Big Foot then had to trace through to show where each of the loans went into which if his three accounts (business, personal, and investment). Ultimately, he did so, even though by this time he was a nervous wreck. Begrudgingly, the tax agent allowed another offset of $215,000 against the $395,000 discrepancy. This third-time revised discrepancy now stood at $180,000 . . . still a lot of additional tax potential.

Big Foot recalled that several of his T-bills matured that year, and that he had redeemed some mutual fund shares. He wasn't sure of the total amount, but thought is was around $150,000. The problem was he didn't have his confirmation statements. Nor was he sure into which of his three accounts (business, personal, or investment) the money was deposited. After contacting and recontacting his brokerage firm, he got duplicate confirmation that three T-bills matured for $120,000 and that two mutual fund redemptions amounted to $27,269. Because they were in even amounts, he was able to trace the T-bill deposits rather easily. Being odd-figure amounts, the two mutual fund deposits were more difficult. In fact, he never did find any exact match. However, he found two deposit amounts that were within a few hundred dollars of the two redemption checks. Seeing that Big Foot was really trying, the tax agent allowed $147,000 offset against the $180,000 discrepancy. The residual discrepancy was now down to $33,000.

Suddenly, Big foot remembered that he loaned his brother $25,000 several years ago. There was no written promissory payback note to this effect. But his wife remembered depositing the $25,000 payback in their personal checking account. This deposit was easily identified . . . BUT. How could the tax agent be sure that the $25,000 wasn't "skim money" that Big Foot took from his business? The brother had to be called in. He was asked to make a written declaration "Under penalties of perjury" that he indeed borrowed $25,000 from Big Foot. The brother also had to produce his own financial records showing where and when he deposited the money. In a sense of desperation, the tax agent allowed the $25,000 offset against the $33,000 discrepancy. He said, however, "This is it! No more! You have taken six weeks of my time and my supervisor is pressing me to close the case."

At this point, Big Foot, too, was weary. The unexplained discrepancy was now down to $8,000. (This was less than 3% of his $294,000 reported income.) Reluctantly, he consented to the $8,000 being tax treated as an "income deficiency." This meant that he would have to pay additional tax. Better on $8,000 than on $542,000!

Throughout the six-week ordeal, Big Foot never slept soundly. Many a night he woke up in a cold sweat trying to recall his various deposit transactions. "It was a hellish nightmare," he said. "I'll never go through that again. I've learned my lesson."

How to Start Right

Big Foot, like so many other entrepreneurs who became successful, never took seriously the stories he heard of others who had their bank deposits tax examined. His conscience was clear . . . but not his depository trails.

So, what are the lessons that Big Foot learned? There are five that could benefit you, namely—

First. When in business, have only one business account and do not involve it with other accounts that you may control. Keep the business account in a separate depository institution from all others. You want it so isolated that every deposit to it can be separately traced.

Second. The number of depository accounts under your control should be no more than three at any one time. These should be:

(1) a business account (checking only)
(2) a personal account (checking/savings)
(3) an investment account (checking/savings)

Preferably, each account should be in a separate depository institution of its own. This is to avoid similarity of monthly statements and practices. This is also to avoid the compounding of computer and interoffice foul-ups by an "all-accounts-in-one" financial establishment.

A "depository account" is one in which you place money with the expectation of withdrawing and disbursing that money frequently throughout the year. This includes trading and rollover accounts. Long-term investments and long-term loans are not depository in nature.

Third. Identify every deposit or group of deposits by its tax *character*. Make separate deposits for each separate tax character. Obtain — and keep — the deposit confirmations; mark on your copy the tax character of each. We list in Figure 5.1 the tax character of those deposits most likely to occur in a small or medium-sized business. Your experience may uncover others. Avoid being a collection agent or check cashier for other people's money.

Fourth. At the deposit entries on every monthly bank statement, make a notation cross-referencing them to the deposit confirmation documents that you have. Index and file the deposit confirmations in a separate system, along the lines indicated in Figure 5.1. You want immediate access to those confirmations when the tax attack come.

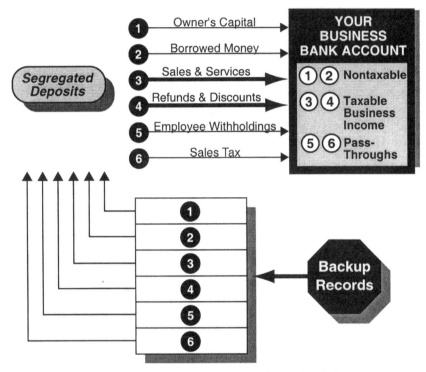

Fig. 5.1 - Character of Deposits Into Business Bank Account

Fifth. At the end of each tax year, tally the total deposits in all (three) of your bank accounts. Compare this with the total positive income reported on your personal and business tax returns. Reconcile any discrepancy promptly. Don't wait until several years after the fact, when the IRS comes on the scene.

Why do we say 3-only depository accounts? Because the human mind associates more readily with distinctions among three items than among five, seven, or other.

Our depiction of a 3-only banking scheme is presented in Figure 5.2. Note that each account is in a separate financial institution of its own. This forces you to consciously make a decision — and make a paper trail — when you transfer money between accounts.

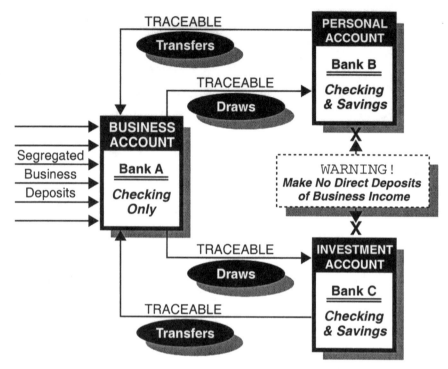

Fig. 5.2 - Banking Discipline With 3-Only Accounts

"Big Stub" Business Checks

The IRS tax letter to Big Foot (in our nightmarish example above) also included the following demand:

All records and books to determine deductions, expenses, tax credits, and prepayment credits: invoices, canceled checks, cash receipts, contracts, escrows, statements, diary, calendar, travel logs, policies for insurance, tax bills, inventory records, worksheets, and any other records used to determine deductions and expenses.

For our purposes at the moment, the key item in the above paragraph that we want to focus on is *canceled checks*. When you are in business, and you disburse money from your business bank account, your canceled checks are unsurpassed for establishing "proof of payment." This is because they are third-party documents. They have been processed through the banking system in a manner over which you had no control. Canceled checks are prima facie evidence of transactional facts. You want these canceled checks in your permanent records.

Good canceled-check practices require that your business checks be large in size: both the check and its stub. We call these "big stub" checks. You want enough space and lines to write (or type) descriptive notes and cross references. Ideally, you want the check and its stub to be self-explanatory when you have to tax-hunt for them three to five years down the road.

Commercial banks and accounting-form designers have all sorts of check-writing recordkeeping schemes. We suggest that you examine several, and select the scheme that best fits your particular business. But don't get too fancy. We don't want you to be a slave to bank deposits and accounting mechanics. All you want is to be able to identify, by cross-referencing to other documents, every disbursement check that you write. Prenumbered checks and prenumbered stubs are very helpful in this regard, but screw-ups can still occur.

The ideal scheme, we think, consists of three essential elements. These elements are:

1. A coding/indexing system that correlates with the itemized expenditures on your business tax return.
2. A means (big stubs, full ledgers, check journals) for systematically recording each prenumbered check as it is written, with a code/index number hand-entered thereon.
3. A sequential easy-to-retrieve hard copy file of the canceled checks, as they are returned from the bank.

Since this is not an accounting book (it is a "tax guide"), we want to stress the protective elements involved but not the particulars. Towards this end, we present Figure 5.3. Note that in the codifying index — and on the canceled checks themselves —

we are trying to key into *every line entry* on your business tax schedules. If you make this tie-in as you go along, you'll have sleepful nights when the tax wolf growls.

YOUR CHECKBOOK

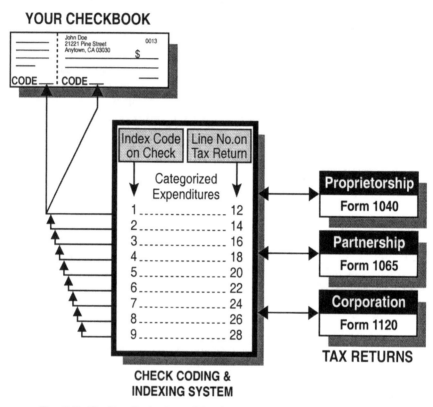

**CHECK CODING &
INDEXING SYSTEM**

Fig. 5.3 - Coding/Indexing of Business Expenses to Tax Returns

How you keep your personal checking and investment/savings accounts is up to you. Just be sure that you do *not* pay any business expenditures from those accounts. If you advance money to, or transfer it from, your business account, do so in even-dollar increments (in $100 or $1,000 amounts) . . . with clear paper trails.

Cash and Barter?

There is one subject on which little is written, but which is on every tax agent's mind. All that green-cash you received in your business; what did you do with it? How do you account for it? And what about all that bartering you do? Do you report it?

Some tax agents have fanciful imaginations about bundles of cash coming in which you are skimming off. Without specific facts, they can't directly accuse you of this. But they are thinking about it all of the time: cash and barter. They deftly try to catch you off guard, then pounce on you.

On the other hand, some businesses are quite susceptible. For example, restaurants, neighborhood retail stores, beauty salons, handyman shops, repair services, landscape maintenance, independent contractors, and the like are vulnerable. In these businesses, cash is king and barter is queen. Some probably are part of the underground economy.

If you are in a "suspected business" where cash and bartering are common, you must prepare a *cash journal.* Whether you enter every 10-cent transaction or not is your affair. But you'd better make some entries. Enter the date, amount, name of person, and purpose of the transaction. Enter the cash received, cash paid out, barter value received, and barter value given. A cash journal, more or less kept up to date, is generally accepted as evidence of your good faith in trying to accurately record your business income.

Here's our rule-of-thumb on the keeping of cash journals. If your cash and bartering transactions are truly less than 5% of your otherwise gross sales and/or receipts for the year, forget about a cash journal. If you were to prepare one in which your cash and barter receipts turned out to be, say, 3%, a tax agent would suspect that you were not keeping a full and correct record.

On the other hand, if your cash and barter receipts do reach 5% or more of your gross for the year, we strongly advise you to keep such a journal. If you do not, the IRS will impute to you an unreported cash amount based on its statistical studies of businesses similar to yours. Where cash is customary and you have no cash journal, you are in no position to dispute the IRS.

The "De Minimis" Rule

Why are we so confident of our 5% no-cash-journal threshold? Because of the *de minimis rule* in the tax code. This rule appears not too clearly in Section 132(e) (employee fringe benefits) and in

Section 280A(g) (certain rental use). In tax jargon, the term "de minimis" means—

Any property or service the value of which is . . . so small as to make accounting for it unreasonable or administratively impractical. [Sec. 132(e)(1)]

We can find no actual percentage figure in the tax code. However, Section 280A(g) uses the phrase—

less than 15 days during the taxable year . . . shall not be included in the gross income.

This excerpt relates to the de minimis rental of one's personal residence (while on vacation, etc.). The resulting fraction is 15/365 which is 4.11% (exactly). Hence, we are interpreting "less than 5%" as constituting de minimis.

Whether de minimis or not, all cash received in a business is supposed to be tax reported. How do you do this if no cash journal is maintained? You simply deposit it in your business bank account along with your other deposits.

Every bank has its deposit slips designed to accommodate cash amounts. There is a CASH line on the deposit form. This line is sub-lined into two parts: currency and coin. If, throughout the year, you had at least a few of your (confirmed) deposit slips with cash entries, you have a third-party documentation in your favor. This should keep an overzealous tax agent from guessing what your cash receipts might have been. Because of this "cash craze" by the IRS, many merchants prefer credit card receipts to cash.

Borrowed Money

Most every business, particularly when starting new, needs to borrow money to keep its operation going. Borrowed money is *not* taxable income. The concern, however, is that the borrowed money is added to and commingled with taxable income of the business. This causes the depository tracing problem that we discussed earlier. Unless a borrowed deposit is positively traceable to its lending source, you can wind up paying income tax on it.

There are two classes of borrowed money: commercial and noncommercial. Commercial lenders are banks and financial institutions; noncommercial lenders are family and friends. In a sense, owner's capital also is a form of borrowed money. But it has the element of risk that lender money does not have.

New businesses tend to be lax in keeping all forms of borrowed money separately identified. Our position is that *every act of borrowing* (including owner capital) should be separately documented. In this regard, automatic lines of credit can be a disservice. Automatic credit is a blending of rollovers of one loan into another, then into another . . . and so on. We suggest some system of "controlled access" to this credit. You want to know exactly when each advance is made, and how much. Line-of-credit running accounts often are difficult to decipher when a deposits-tracing tax agent is breathing down your neck.

Tracing the origin of noncommercial loans can be a real bear. Often, family and friends write out a check and turn it over to the borrower. He then deposits it in his business account. Because of mutual trust, neither takes the time to prepare any documentation on the terms of their agreement. Seldom is any straight-forward promissory note ever written.

Promissory notes are so common that preprinted forms are available in the legal forms section of office supply stores. These preprinted forms contain all of the "promise to pay" legal wording. They also contain blank spaces for entering the amount of principal borrowed, the terms of repayment, rate of interest, due date, and name(s) of the borrower(s). Promissory notes do not have to be notarized, but they can be. Anyone in business should have a pad of promissory notes among his stationery supplies. When a non-commercial loan is consummated with your handshake, whip out a blank promissory note and fill it in. This is an easy way to document the act. It can save you many tax headaches later.

Never Touch OPTM

The letters "OPTM" stand for: *Other People's Tax Money.* There are two forms of OPTM: [1] Sales tax, and [2] Employee withholdings. The sales tax is that which you collect when selling or servicing products at retail (Chapter 3). The employee withholdings are income tax, social security tax, and medicare tax that you withhold from the compensation you pay to employees (Chapter 4). These tax monies belong to those from whom you collect. They are not your money, nor are they monies generated by the business itself. They are NEVER TOUCH money that passes through your hands.

What happens, usually, is that the OPTM is routinely deposited in the business bank account. It is mixed in with ordinary business income with no separate depository distinction. This inflates the cash balance on hand. Unthinkingly, it is made available for other expenditures for the business. When the statutory clock comes due for turning the OPTM over to the proper tax agencies, the OPTM is not there. New money has to be borrowed for taxes. Thus, unconsciously, the vicious money-cycle commences for getting further and further behind.

Depending on the magnitude of OPTM collected, some businesses open a separate tax account. This is not a bad idea, particularly if you have other tax monies that need to be set aside. This is certainly true of an employer's 50% matching of the social security/medicare tax and full payment of federal/state unemployment tax. All employee-employer tax matters are regarded as "trust fund taxes" where a 100% trust recovery penalty applies [IRC Sec. 6672(a)]. This 100% penalty is imposed on the *responsible person* in a business whose duty it is to collect, account for, and pay over the trust fund taxes. Liability for payment of the 100% penalty reaches beyond the business assets to the personal assets of the owner(s) thereof. Trust fund taxes (OPTMs), by the way, are not dischargeable in bankruptcy.

6

OTHER PREBUSINESS ITEMS

> There Are 5 Forms Of Ordinary Endeavor In Business, Namely: Proprietorship, Partnership, Limited Liability Company (LLC), S Corporation, And C Corporation. Before One Form Is Elected, A Business Name, Logo, And Address Need Adoption, As Well As A Projected Starting Date, Accounting Year (Calendar Or Fiscal), And Accounting Method (Cash Or Accrual). Before Serious Start-Up Planning Can Proceed, Serious Cash Money Must Be On Hand By You And Your Associates (If Any). A Federal EIN Needs To Be Obtained, After Which You Notify The IRS Of Your Intentions Via Form 8832: "Entity Classification Election."

We consider Chapters 1 through 5 as our *Tax Psyche Test.* If you have waded through these chapters and found them informative and challenging, rather than intimidating and discouraging, you have passed our "psyche test." You are now in a better position to start a prosperous business of your own. Every business will face taxation issues: federal, state, and local. There is no escaping this reality. What we have tried to do in the preceding chapters is to prepare you mentally for what may lie ahead, before you actually start your own business.

Even though you may be psychologically ready to start a business, there are a number of other items and tasks you must do. These items differ from those previously covered in that, once you have made decisions on them, you seldom have to revisit those decisions. We're talking about selecting a business name and logo, selecting a business form (proprietorship, partnership, LLC, S or C corporation), opening a nonpersonal bank account (with your own money), deciding on cash vs. accrual method of accounting, publishing your business name and activity, and a host of other pesky and mundane matters. For example, one of your mundane tasks is to apply for a Federal Tax ID or EIN (Employer/Entity Identification Number). An EIN for a business is like an SSN (Social Security Number) for an individual. Once assigned, an EIN stays with the business until that business formally terminates.

The decisions you may make on the items covered in this chapter are not forever cast in concrete. For good reason and cause, any decision can be changed. For example, you decide to start a partnership with two like-minded close friends. After a few trial years, the arrangement does not work out. In such a situation, you could change your partners, change the form of business, or change the line of products or services you offer. Our suggestion is that, whatever you decide, start slow, think smart, be methodical, and document your money trails.

Common Forms of Business

These days, there are *five* common forms of business that can be created or acquired by one or more owners thereof. There are: (1) the proprietorship form, (2) the partnership form, (3) the limited liability company (LLC), (4) the S-type corporation, and (5) the C-type corporation. All are tax recognized by the IRS. These "entity forms," as we call them, are also recognized by state franchising and local licensing agencies. As you will see in subsequent chapters, each business form is identified by a separate income tax return (form) of its own. No one form of business enjoys any significant tax advantage over that of any other form.

The choice of one business form over another depends on the type of business to be launched. The choice also depends on the customary practices of others in a similar type business. Public expectations play some role, but such role is not absolute. More importantly, the manner of ownership and the financial needs of the emerging business are far more decision controlling.

By far the simplest form of new business is the sole proprietorship. It is simple because there is only one owner: the creator. This one owner may also be a husband and wife. (A husband and wife are treated as one taxpayer: not two.) The startup capital and follow-through come from the personal savings of the creator, and/or borrowings from family members and close friends. Or, equity lines of credit can be set up against other nonbusiness assets of the creator. Whatever the source of money, there is one-owner control over the business. The business succeeds or fails on the expertise, intelligence, and drive of this one owner. He, she, or both accrue all profits . . . and suffer all losses. When losses happen, livelihoods change.

At the other end of the operational spectrum is the C-type corporation (or "C corp." for short). A C corporation is one in which the business is owned by a group of persons called: shareholders. A small business corporation may consist of five (or fewer) shareholders to as many as 35 (or more). By "small" we mean a corporation whose initial capitalization is at least $1,000,000 (1 million), but not more than $10,000,000 (10 million). The shareholders have "voting power" in proportion to the dollar value of their shares. The shareholders elect a chief executive to run the business, and may also elect other principal operating officers. The officers get a salary for their personal services, whereas the shareholders get a "dividend" if the business succeeds. Corporations, usually, can raise more capital than proprietorships or partnerships.

The point that we are trying to make here is this: The form of business that you select will depend on the number of owners and their contributions of capital. As more owners become involved, operational complexity increases. A one-owner company is more flexible and resilient to change than is a 35-owner company. New businesses are always plagued with unforeseens and the need to change and modify. For this reason, multi-owner companies can do more things. They can create new products and services, take more risks, and they can make more money. As they do, they are challenged more by tax gamesmanship than by livelihood needs.

Sound pro-and-con judgment is required when selecting one initial form of business over another. Thus, instead of trying to present the pros and cons of five forms of businesses in this chapter, we devote a separate subsequent chapter to each of the five. For your road map in this regard, we present Figure 6.1.

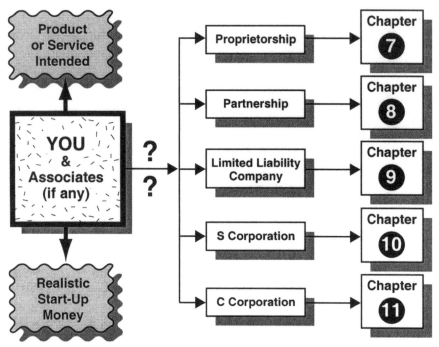

Fig. 6.1 - Upcoming Chapters for Entity Pros & Cons

Based on conversations with your colleagues and/or on the writings of others, you may have already decided (more or less) on your initial form of business. If so, via Figure 6.1, you can go directly to that chapter which is of immediate interest to you. Compare what we say with that which others have said (or have written). It is also possible that you may want to compare the features of other forms of business to the one that you have predecided on. Later in this chapter, we tell you about formalizing your entity selection.

Open Temporary Account(s)

On the supposition that you (and your associates, if any) will be selecting some initial business form, there are certain supporting items that you should be thinking about. Foremost is the opening of a temporary business bank account. We say "temporary" for a very practical reason. If you intend to invite others to join in your venture, you want to show them that you are financially serious. The best way to do this is to open a separate account and get some good faith money into it. A token deposit of a few thousand dollars is quite insufficient when preparing to start a business. Depending on the nature of the business you envision, you should deposit at least $50,000 into that account . . . preferably $100,000. This is not spendable money just yet. It is: "I'm serious" money.

Where does this serious money come from? It comes from your own resources: your savings, sale of investment assets, equity in your home, and/or borrowings from family members. If you really intend to start a business, you want upfront money on hand, in the bank, and ready to use. This means a checking-only account; forgo any interest on that money for the time being.

There is also another reason for such an account. It is for "matching purposes" by other associates who may agree to join with you. A qualifying candidate must either exact-match, near-match, or above-match what you have in your account. If a potential associate is going to smooth talk you into accepting his business contacts, pledges against junk property, or offer of an unsecured promissory note as the equivalent of your serious money, WATCH OUT! Persons who want to join you with no real money of their own on the line tend to be irresponsible with your money. The only real test of the seriousness of an associate is for that person to show money on the line.

What name do you open your bank account under? Use your real name, then add "& Associates." For example, suppose your real name is John J. Jones. (This is a purely fictitious selection on our part.) Your temporary business account name would be—

John J. Jones & Associates

Use your home address or a P.O. Box. You establish the account with your sole signature authority for withdrawals. After all, it is your money (and no one else's) at this point.

If an associate wants to join with you, have him or her open a similar temporary checking account. Preferably do so at another bank. Have that person use an account such as—

Sandra S. Smith & Associates

(This is another fictitious name for illustration purposes only.)

If there is a third, fourth, or fifth associate who wants to join you, have each do likewise as above. For communicative reasons, limit the number of temporary associates to five (you plus four). Get together informally and compare each other's check-writing ability. Make it clear that you will go forward only with those who can demonstrate that they have serious money earmarked and set aside. Ignore those who promise such money later.

For those who have the serious money, set up a schedule of informal meetings to discuss the items that we depict in Figure 6.2. Your objective is to get the preparatory pesky matters out of the way, so that you can launch with full concentration on profit-seeking endeavors.

Business Name & Logo

Every new business needs a name. Select one that is intriguing, yet reasonably self-explanatory. Avoid cutesy names and those that do not convey an instant message. You want instant "name recognition": something that foretells the nature of the business you are offering.

For example, suppose you are going to start a printing business. A possible name could be "Great Impressions." But what does this convey to an ordinary person not familiar with your business? Great Impressions; so what! How about "Town & Country Printing." The "Town & Country" phrase implies that the business serves a widespread area. Or, include your own name and call it "Jones Quality Printing." Or, call it "Pony Express Printing."

The point is that you want to pick a name that is pleasant sounding, while simultaneously giving a short description of the nature of your business. To get ideas in this regard, look in the yellow pages of the phone book(s) in your area. Look up in the index your type of business, then scan the pages for competitor names. But don't try to lock horns with some competitor already in business by using a name closely resembling his.

While scanning the yellow pages, look for small advertising agencies and commercial art services. It is a good idea to contact these businesses for creative assistance. Let them help you select a name and design a logo especially for you.

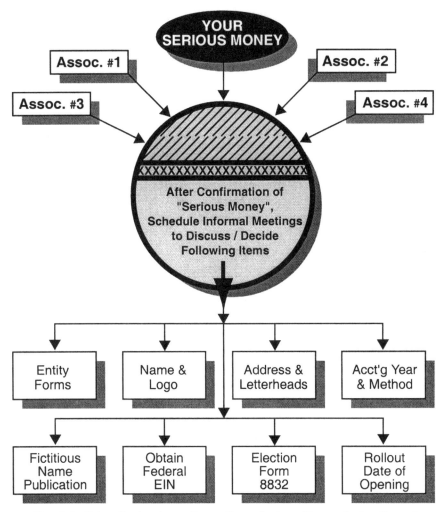

Fig. 6.2 - Other Prebusiness Items Once Serious Money is Confirmed

A logo is a trademark or identifying symbol. It should evolve artistically from the name that you select. It may derive from one of the letters in your name, or from the initials, or by symbolizing the lead words used. For example, "Pony Express Printing" could have as its logo the initials P-E-P in some sort of a symbol, or the idea of a racing pony. Get a commercial artist enthused about your new business idea, and together you and he (or she) will come up with a name and logo that will please you.

Should you trademark register your name and logo? That all depends. Trademark registration covers names, titles, short expressions, service marks, and symbols that identify or distinguish goods and services being offered to the public. It is a good idea to register your name and logo if you expect to sell your business at some point down the road. A TM-registered name and logo becomes a capital asset. It increases in value with time — known as "goodwill" — as the business prospers. If interested in TM registration, contact the Commissioner of Patents and Trademarks, Washington, D.C. 20231.

Initial Address & Letterheads

A common entrepreneurial mistake is to sign a one-to-five year lease for office and shop space in a prestigious business section of town. Yes, you may have the money on the line to do so. But once you sign a legal contract, you are bound by the terms of the contract, whether your business makes money or loses it.

Our suggestion is: Be frugal. Why not rent a P.O. Box, instead. Many businesses, large and small, use a P.O. Box address, often long after the business is up and running . . . and successful. A P.O. Box address is highly acceptable for all forms of written business communications, including licenses and permits, federal and state tax returns, vendor and supplier billings, marketing and sales flyers, and so on. Treat such an address as temporary until you get more firmly established.

If you need a secretarial service with phone, fax, Internet, and e-mail services, *rent* such a service. Do so at least initially. Similarly, if you need handling and storage space, rent a cubicle from a local storage rental service. If you need certain types of nonhighway equipment, rent that also. But, whatever you need, use the shortest rental measuring time that you can: hour, day, week, or month. The advantage of renting certain assets — at least initially — is that once productive income comes in, rental expenditures can be expensed whereas capital expenditures have to be amortized and/or depreciated (recall Chapter 2).

After settling on your name, logo, and initial business address, get your business stationery printed up. This includes letterheads, envelopes, business cards, customer receipts, sales invoices, fee statements, and the like. Use your name and logo in different sizes and type fonts as appropriate. While the name and logo are a capital asset (not tax deductible as an operating expense), printed stationery is an operating expense. It is fully tax deductible in the year that you commence business.

Fictitious Name Publication

You are now approaching the stage where you want to announce the availability of your business to the public. A "start-first" way to do this is to register your business name with the county clerk where your principal operations will be. Then you publish your "fictitious name" in the legal notices section in a leading newspaper in your area. It is fictitious only in the sense that your full personal name is not used. It is, or will be, a locally registered business name.

A fictitious name publication is a sure-fire way of putting local taxing agencies and licensing authorities on notice. These agencies and authorities have staff personnel whose job is to look for these notices. When they see a new business name in print, they send out a prepackage of official application forms, rules and regulations, and threats of penalties if you do not contact their offices immediately. If a particular application form applies in your case, by all means complete it and return it. If a fee is required, attach the fee. Use the minimum fee that is indicated on the fee schedule included in the prepackage.

If an application form does not fit your case, write across it in big, bold, red letters: NOT APPLICABLE. Date and sign your name, and return it in the envelope provided or to the address indicated. If you do not do this, there will be follow-up demands, and the penalty threats will get larger and bolder.

In addition, upon publication of your fictitious name, you will receive advertising fliers from vendors, suppliers, salesmen, accountants, attorneys, consultants, and others. Save those that appeal to you, as you may need their services later.

Once in a while, your fictitious name notice will produce a "cease and desist" order by some legal firm representing an unknown competitor. Out of just pure coincidence, that competitor's name and logo may be similar to yours. If this occurs, contact the law firm for further particulars. If there is truly a close similarity, go back to your commercial artist and rename and redesign. Often, only minor changes are necessary.

There is legal purpose to your fictitious name publication. It causes you to "go on record" as to the personal name(s) of the owner(s) of the business, the official business address, the general nature of the business intended, and its "opening date." Set this date 30, 60 or 90 days in advance to allow adequate time for unpaid creditors and unpaid tax collectors to come forward. Nothing is more embarrassing or more demoralizing to the owner(s) of a newly-formed business than having a uniformed sheriff show up with a court order for the collection of an unpaid debt. Even worse is having the sheriff or IRS collections agent show up while you are in direct personal contact with a prospective customer or client.

The moral here is obvious. If you or any of your co-owners have creditor debts or tax delinquencies outstanding, you must clear them up before starting business. You'll have enough financial accounting and tax tasks to attend to, without carrying old baggage from the past.

Federal EIN Number

One agency that will not respond to your fictitious name notice (there may be others) is the Internal Revenue Service (IRS). You have to contact it; it will not contact you.

Look in the front of your phone book for government agency listings. Look for the listing: Internal Revenue Service; it's there. Then look for the sublisting: Federal Tax Forms. Call that number (you may have to call it several times). Ask for **Form SS-4**: *Application for Employer Identification Number (EIN)*. You'll be directed to the IRS web site at **www.irs.gov/businesses**. Click on **Employer ID Numbers**. Download the SS-4 and its seven pages of instructions. The form consists of numerous entry lines and some 38 checkboxes. Complete the form as applicable in your case. Sign your name and title, then follow the instructions: *How to Apply* (on line, phone, fax, or mail).

The SS-4 is an *application* for a federal EIN number; it is not a tax form per se. The "SS" stands for Social Security. This means that whatever number is assigned to you by the IRS will be passed along to the Social Security Administration (SSA) for its records. As a new business employer, the SSA will be expecting you to collect social security and medicare taxes from your employees.

An edited arrangement of Form SS-4 is presented in Figure 6.3. We have edited it and rearranged it extensively because we want to call particular attention to those items that are specifically addressed to new businesses.

Note in Figure 6.3 the checkboxes and blank spaces for type of organization, reason for applying, nature of business activity, to whom products and services are intended, and number of business outlets. Note also the questions about principal business location, starting date, anticipated number of employees, type of employees, and first date wages are to be paid. In the lower portion, just above your signature, you are expressly asked:

Has the applicant ever applied for an identification number for this or any other business? ☐ *Yes* ☐ *No*
If "Yes," enter name and trade name. Also enter approximate date, city and state where the application was filed, and previous number if known.

The instructions accompanying Form SS-4 tell you that every time you change the name of your business or its principal locations, you have to notify the IRS. The instructions also tell you that every time you change your *form* of business — proprietorship to partnership, or partnership to corporation, or vice versa — you have to apply for a **new** EIN.

After processing your application, you will receive a—

NOTICE OF NEW EMPLOYER
IDENTIFICATION NUMBER ASSIGNED

The number assigned will be indicated in the upper right-hand corner of the IRS notice. The text of the notice will read, in part—

The number above has been assigned to you. We will use it to identify your business tax returns and any other related documents, even if you have no employees. . . . Use the number and your name exactly as shown above on all

Federal tax forms that require this information, and refer to the number in all tax payments and in tax-related correspondence or documents.

Form SS - 4 — APPLICATION FOR EMPLOYER IDENTIFICATION NUMBER

Name & Trade Name

Address: Principal Place of Business

Other Mailing Address

Your true name - if proprietorship

Managing partner's name - if partnership

Principal officer's name - if corporation

Ending month of tax year — mo ▶ / yr ▶

Type of business	☐ Proprietorship ☐ Partnership ☐ Corporation
Nature of principal activity:	
Peak number of employees in next 12 months ▲	
Type of employees	☐ Nonagricultural ☐ Agricultural ☐ Domestic

Reason for applying: ☐ Starting new ☐ Purchased business ☐ Other _____

Principal product & raw material used:

First date wages will be paid: mo / day / yr

Selling to whom: ☐ Businesses ☐ General public ☐ Other _____

More than one place of business? ☐ yes ☐ no

Starting date of business: mo / day / yr

Have you ever applied before? ☐ yes *(if "yes", give particulars)* _____ ☐ no

Signature	Date	Title	Phone No.

Fig. 6.3 - Highly Edited Arrangement of Form SS-4

As a precautionary measure, we suggest that you file the SS-4 application approximately 60 days before you open your doors to the public. This will give you time to browse through the "Employer's Tax Guide" that the IRS will send you, plus other tax forms and instructions. This will also allow you time to set up your business bank account properly. You will have to supply to the bank your EIN, even if you have no employees.

Accounting Year & Method

Although not shown in Figure 6.3, on the official SS-4 there is a mid-page item captioned:

Closing month of accounting year.

What the IRS is looking for is that you designate the month — that is, the end of the month — that coincides with the end of the adopted taxable year of your business operation. If your initial entity selection is other than a C corporation, it is best that you use a calendar year. In this case, your "closing month" would be December. If you elect to be a C corporation, you could adopt a fiscal year. In this case, your closing month could be any month except December. However, if you have employees, the preferable fiscal year closing months are March, June, and September. Said months are more compatible with your filings of Employer Quarterly Returns. (Recall page 4-10 in Chapter 4.)

As to method of accounting, this refers to cash vs. accrual vs. some other acceptable method. The term "method" is how you post your books of account for receipts and disbursements throughout the operational year. Professional accountants love to haggle over this feature and have you adopt the accrual method. C corporations with gross receipts of more than $10,000,000 (10 million) are required to use the accrual method. But you are not there yet in terms of gross receipts.

Be informed now of IRC Section 448(b)(3): **Limitation on Use of Cash Method of Accounting; Exception;** *Entities with Gross Receipts of Not More Than $5,000,000.* There is a further exception to this exception in Revenue Procedure 2002-28. This latest IRS procedure permits small businesses whose average annual gross receipts for the prior three years are $10,000,000 or less to use the *cash method* of accounting.

The cash method is simpler and makes more common sense. Suppose, for example, that you have delivered a product or have performed a service for a customer or client in the month of November. You bill that person a few days later. He pays you in January of the following year. On the cash basis, you report the income in January. On the accrual basis, you report the income in November. If your accounting year ends in December, under the accrual method you would be paying tax on money you have not received. This one feature alone — paying tax on money that you have not received — does not sit well with new business owners.

Furthermore, if you do not receive the money in January (under the accrual method) you have to file a lawsuit to try to collect it. After trial, a Court Order for payment is issued. Unless the debtor pays voluntarily your billed amount plus court costs and legal fees, the collection order has to be served upon the debtor by a uniformed Sheriff. If the debtor has left town, you have to track him down and engage a Sheriff in another jurisdiction to make service. You have to endure this kind of procedure before the IRS will let you write off the money that you paid tax on as a *business bad debt.* Several years can go by.

Under the cash method, you can file a lawsuit for collection action if you want to. But, since you haven't actually received the money, you do not pay tax on it prematurely. Consequently, our position is that, until you are IRS compelled to use the accrual method (as required for C corporations and tax shelters), the cash method should be your books-of-accounting choice. Interestingly, it leads also to better tax discipline.

Entity Class Election

There is still one more item that you need to know about, before commencing business. This item is called: *Entity Classification Election* — Form 8832. The purpose of this form is to put the IRS on notice as to which business entity form you have chosen, its effective date for business starting, and who is the initial spokesperson for the business. An abridged format of Form 8832 is presented in Figure 6.4. As you can readily note, the headportion requires your business name, address, and EIN. As you can also note, there are six specific items designated, namely:

Form 8832	ENTITY CLASSIFICATION ELECTION	
	Name of entity _____ Address: city or town, state, ZIP	**EIN**
1	**Type of election** **a** ☐ Initial classification: newly-formed **b** ☐ Change in current classification	

2	**Form of entity (elected)**
	● Domestic elegible entities
	   a☐ b☐ c☐
	● Foreign eligible entities
	   d☐ e☐ f☐	

3	**Disregarded entity information** **a** Name of owner ▶ _____ **b** Owner's Tax ID ▶ _____ **c** Country of organization ▶ _____	
4 **5** **6**	Beginning effective date ▶ _____ month / day / year _____ Name of spokesperson ▶ _____ That person's phone number ▶ ( ) _____	
CONSENT STATEMENT & SIGNATURE(S)		
Signature(s)	Date	Title

Fig. 6.4 - Abbreviated Contents of Entity Election Form 8832

1. *Type of election* (2 checkboxes)

2. *Form of entity elected* (6 checkboxes)

3. *Disregarded entity information*

BEFORE STARTING A BUSINESS

4. *Beginning date of entity* (month, day, year)

5. *Name of person for IRS contact*

6. *Phone number of contact person*

For those reading this book, the most likely type of election would be **1a**: *A newly-formed entity.* As such, you need to think through carefully what your elected starting date would be. Whatever that date, you had better be ready to start your books of accounting on that date. We urge, therefore, that you get all of your prebusiness chores out of the way — including your selection of initial entity form (from Chapters 7 through 11 which follow) — before filing Form 8832.

There are three pages of official instructions that accompany Form 8832. One of the more intriguing of these instructions is the paragraph captioned: ***Disregarded entity.*** This paragraph reads:

> *A disregarded entity is an eligible entity* [which is not automatically a corporation by law] *that is treated as an entity that is not separate from its single* [sole] *owner. Its separate existence will be ignored for Federal tax purposes unless it elects corporate tax treatment.*

The concept of a "disregarded entity" is directed at single member LLCs (Limited Liability Companies). For a sole owner of a business to be treated as an entity, he/she must elect corporate status (for federal purposes). For most state tax purposes, a special LLC tax return form is provided. We'll get to LLC matters more fully in Chapter 9: Limited Liability Company.

Every member in a newly-formed entity must sign the ***Consent Statement*** at the bottom of Form 8832. Each member's consent is made *Under penalties of perjury.* No consent and no Form 8832 are required if one self-elects to be a sole proprietorship (without limited liability) or if two or more owners agree to be a general partnership (without limited liability). In the following chapters, we address *domestic* eligible entities only.

7

PROPRIETORSHIP: FORM 1040

> For A Proprietorship, Schedule C (1040) Is Where All The Action Is. This Is Your Basic Profit Or Loss Statement On Which Some 25 Official Deduction Categories Are Preprinted. There Are Other Associated Forms, The Most Important Being Form 4562 (Depreciation And Amortization) And Schedule SE (Self-Employment Tax). In The Head Portion Of Schedule C There Are Certain Questions And Checkboxes That Must Be Answered. If You Claim Office-In-Home And/Or Car and Truck Expenses, Your "Business Use Percentage" Must Be Established. Travel, Meals, And Entertainment Require Extreme Documentary Detail.

In this chapter, we want to focus exclusively on proprietorships. This is the simplest form of business, and illustrates the basic accounting involvement of any trade or business. Whether you operate as a proprietorship or not, the material in this chapter is a tax prelude to that for partnerships, LLCs, and corporations.

We have in mind two particular areas for discussion. One area is the gamut of tax forms involved. These differ substantially for each form of business. We are not going to fill out the forms; we are just going to tell you which ones are applicable — and why. We will go into some detail, however, into the central (basic) form required. For a proprietorship, this is Schedule C (Form 1040).

Our second area for discussion has to do with selected fully deductible current expenses. We will pick three of these that are highly vulnerable to tax challenge. For proprietorships, these are: (1) office-in-home, (2) car and truck expenses, and (3) travel and entertainment. We will pick other current expenses for in-depth discussion when we get to partnerships, LLCs, and corporations.

There is also another proprietorship schedule that attaches to Form 1040. This is Schedule F: *Profit or Loss from Farming.* This schedule is used by single-family farms, of which there are very few these days. Farm corporations now dominate the agricultural landscape. Consequently, for our expected readers, we will bypass Schedule F in its entirety.

We will stick solely with Schedule C (1040) proprietorship activities. We will not get into other sources of income that you might have, as these may require separate tax forms of their own. Nor will we repeat our discussions in previous chapters. Those previous items apply to all forms of business without exception.

Overview of Forms Required

The existence of Form 1040: ***U.S. Individual Income Tax Return***, is well known. Every individual (married or single) earning income of any kind — from business or otherwise — files this form. The front page of this form is arranged into approximately 15 lines for reporting specific sources of income. One of these 15 lines reads, officially, as follows:

Business income or (loss) (attach Schedule C)

The intended entry, of course, is the *net* profit or loss: **not** the gross receipts or sales.

For proprietorships, therefore, the basic tax form is **Schedule C (Form 1040)**. Its official heading is—

Profit or Loss from Business (Sole Proprietorship)

▶ *Attach to Form 1040*   ▶ *See Instructions*

The very first line entry on Schedule C is *Name of proprietor* (singular). It does not say proprietors (plural). This is important to note. Many husbands and wives in business together think of themselves both as the proprietors of the same business. And, indeed, they may well be. But only one can be named on Schedule C as the sole proprietor. There is a special reason for this. It has to do with the filing of Schedule SE: *Self-Employment Tax*. This is a separate tax on each proprietor. It is a combined form of social security and medicare tax. It is computed on the same net income of Schedule C as that which is reported on page 1 of Form 1040. It is often referred to as the "second" income tax for a proprietor.

For the same husband and wife business, it is possible to file two Schedules C: one "his"; one "hers." The two Schedules C must be treated as separate businesses, each with its own separate books of account. The instructions on this point say—

If you had more than one business, or if you and your spouse had separate businesses, you must complete a Schedule C for each business.

In other words, there is no prohibition against attaching multiple Schedules C to the same Form 1040.

Before we get into other Schedule C details, we should give you a quick overview of all the tax forms associated with Schedule C. This we do in Figure 7.1. Please take a moment to glance at it.

Those form numbers shown in bold in Figure 7.1 are specifically mentioned on Schedule C itself. If they apply, you MUST attach them. There are three such forms, namely: 4562, 8829, and 6198. This is the functional order in which they appear on Schedule C. There are also "other related" forms.

Form 4562 is the *Depreciation and Amortization* form we discussed in Chapter 2 (Deferred Capital Recovery). Virtually every proprietorship (as well as every other form of business) claims a depreciation deduction. In their formative years, many businesses also claim an amortization deduction.

Form 8829 is officially titled: *Expenses for Business Use of Your Home*. Many startup proprietorships use the personal residence of the proprietor as the principal place of business, at least initially. It is economical to do so. However, there are stringent rules for figuring the amount of expense deduction that you are allowed. Form 8829 steps you through these rules in a sequential and methodical manner.

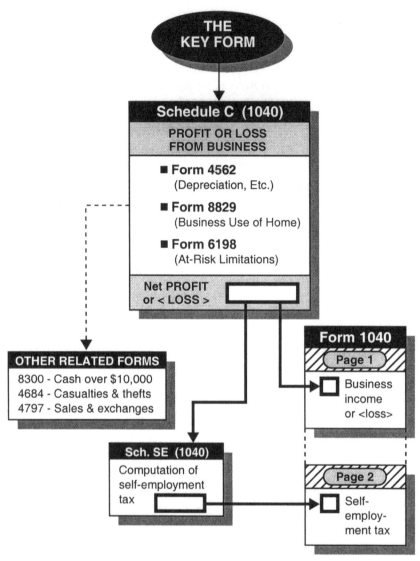

Fig. 7.1 - Tax Forms Associated with a Proprietorship

As to **Form 6198:** *At-Risk Limitations*, Schedule C carries this notice—

If you have a loss, you MUST check the box that describes your investment in this activity:

☐ *All investment is at risk.*

☐ *Some investment is not at risk. Attach Form 6198.*

The phrase "not at risk" means operating your business with borrowed money (loans) that are nonrecourse (unsecured), protected by stop-loss guarantees, or informal advances from family members and/or close business associates. There is nothing tax-wrong with borrowing money to use in your business, so long as you have a legal (enforceable) obligation to pay it back. If you have such obligations, Form 6198 does not apply. Obviously, we are recommending that you position yourself to check the "All . . . at risk" box above.

Other Related Forms

In Figure 7.1 there is reference to three other tax forms. These forms and their official headings are:

Form 8300 — Report of Cash Payments Over $10,000 Received in a Trade or Business

Form 4684 — Casualties and Thefts to Property Used in a Trade or Business

Form 4797 — Gains and Losses from Sales or Exchanges of Assets Used in a Trade or Business and Involuntary Conversions

These forms are as applicable to partnerships, LLCs, and corporations as they are to proprietorships. Each form says, "Attach to your tax return." A few words on each are instructive.

If you receive from a customer, client, or other person (or organization) cash of more than $10,000 in one or more related transactions, you may be required to prepare Form 8300. We say "may be required" because much depends on the nature of the cash received, from whom, for what purpose, and under what circumstances. Form 8300 requires you to detail all of this, including the actual count of the number of $100 bills received.

You do **not** attach Form 8300 to Schedule C. Instead, within 15 days after the cash transaction, you file it with the IRS in Detroit, MI (at the address in the form's instructions).

For Form 8300 purposes, "cash" is defined as coin (gold or silver), U.S. currency, and foreign currency. It is that which is customarily used as *bearer money*. It is that which is accepted on its face value: no signatures required; no guarantees required; no personal references required. The $10,000 count is that which takes place in a 24-hour period with the same person. So, if someone brings large amounts of cash to you, start your clock before you rush off to prepare Form 8300. If it looks like the cash bearer is going to approach the $10,000 figure, direct him to a local bank. Instruct him to bring back to you a cashier's check instead. Cashier's checks, regardless of the amount — could be $1,000,000 or more — do not have to be reported on Form 8300. We think you have more important things to do than being an informant for the IRS on your cash customers.

Form 4684: *Casualties and Thefts* is in two parts. Section A is for personal use property; Section B is for business use property. In either case, you have to describe each property item that is damaged, destroyed, or stolen. You have to take into account the amount of insurance reimbursement, if any. You have to get a professional appraisal of the property "before and after" the casualty, and then you have to compute its change in fair market value. If your insurance reimbursement is greater than the loss in fair market value, you have net taxable income rather than a tax recognized loss.

Form 4684 and the casualty/theft rules therewith are quite complex. Whatever the outcome, the information is not entered on Schedule C. It is entered on Form 4797 and then subsequently onto Form 1040 (either on its page 1 or elsewhere).

Form 4797 is a very special form, far beyond the scope of our discussion here. Its full official title is: *Sales of Business Property (Including Involuntary Conversions and Recapture Amounts)*. Its primary use is when a business is sold, exchanged, bankrupt, or involuntarily converted (by condemnation or threat thereof). Recapture amounts apply to certain items whose business use falls below 50%. Form 4797 is also useful when the major assets of a business are being disposed of. In these situations, you are dealing in *capital* transactions (capital gains and/or capital losses). These are not the ordinary profit or loss activities when starting a new business, regardless of form.

Format/Content of Schedule C

Schedule C (Form 1040) is *the* tax form of concern to every proprietor: whether in a trade, business, or profession. Unless you are in a partnership, LLC, S corporation, or are a full-time employee to someone else in business, Schedule C is the form for you. It is a basic profit-or-loss statement that is useful for other purposes besides tax return filings. You should master this form.

Without the officialese, we present in Figure 7.2 our edited version of Schedule C. We want you to become familiar with its general format and content only. We are showing page 1, as that is where all of the P or L (profit or loss) action is.

In Figure 7.2, we first call your attention to the second line there. The full official wording on that line is—

Principal business or profession, including product or service.
Principal business code.   ▶ _____.

In the instructions to Schedule C is a listing of approximately 175 business activities that the IRS has computer coded. Each activity is assigned a separate 6-digit code. You are told to—

Select the activity code that identifies (or most closely identifies) the business or profession that is the principal source of your sales and receipts.

Obviously, the purpose of this codification is to make it easier for the IRS to computer-match and track your business activities by comparing with others in your same line.

Overall, Schedule C consists of the following parts:

Page 1   **Page 2**

General Information   Part III— Cost of Goods Sold
Part I — Income   Part IV— Information on Vehicles
Part II — Expenses   Part V — Other Expenses

The general information portion consists of about a dozen statements, questions, and checkboxes, such as: *Do you "materially participate" in the operation of this business?* ☐ *Yes*

☐ *No.* These items are designed to test your tax knowledge and expertise. If applicable, make sure you answer correctly.

Schedule C (Form 1040)	PROFIT OR (LOSS): PROPRIETORSHIP	Tax Year
Name	Soc. Sec. No.	
Principal Business	Business Code	
Business Address	Employer I.D.	

////////////////////// General Information //////////////////////

Accounting method	☐ Cash	☐ Accrual	☐ Other
Inventory method	☐ Cost	☐ Lower	☐ Other

	Yes	No
¥ Any change in closing inventory?		
¥ Did you "materially participate"?		
¥ Any deduction for office-in-home?		
¥ File all employer quarterly returns?		
¥ Still in business at end of year?		

Part I   Income //

Gross receipts or sales .... _____

- _____   _____
- _____   _____
- _____   _____
- _____   _____

Your total income > > > > > > > > > > > > > > [_____]

Part II   Expenses //

(See Fig. 7.3)   (See Fig. 7.4)

Other expenses (specify)

---------------------- _____
---------------------- _____
---------------------- _____

Total Expenses ▶ [_____]

NET PROFIT OR (LOSS) ▶ [_____]

Fig. 7.2 - General Format/Content of Schedule C (1040)

In Part II, there are approximately 25 official expense deduction lines. We have taken liberty in Figure 7.3 to alphabetize and redesignate the lines into a 3-digit sequence of numbers. We also have added some short explanatory wording. We have done this so that you might use the digit sequencing for coding into your own system of accounts. The proper coding of allowable (current expense) deductions is crucial to your tax survival. If you are careless or sloppy in these matters, you *will* pay a price.

Office-in-Home Deduction

Near the bottom of Schedule C (on page 1), there is a deduction line entry that reads—

Expenses for business use of your home. Attach **Form 8829**.

We want to tell you about the office-in-home deduction.

Many proprietorship businesses do have an office in home. This helps to cut down overhead. But more importantly, proprietorship businesses usually require an owner's attention 12 to 16 hours a day. One needs the privacy and quiet of his home to do his thinking, planning, worrying, and posting of books of account. An office in home is also useful for seeing clients, interviewing employees, discussions with sales/advertising staff, storing valuable inventory, and conducting other business transactions that are impractical to conduct in the open marketplace (where security may be of concern).

In any bona fide business, expenses associated with an office are fully deductible. With an office in home, however, the implication is that it is used for personal purposes as well. Because of this implication, special rules have been enacted (Sec. 280A) to deny certain expense deductions when there is an operating loss from the business.

Section 280A of the tax code is titled: ***Disallowance of Certain Expenses in Connection with Business Use of Home.*** This section is a general prohibition against claiming office-in-home expenses. It is targeted primarily at employees (engineers, teachers, salespersons, programmers) and part-time entrepreneurs in hobbies, sports, recreational activities, investments, and direct sales. Indirectly, it raises the question: What is your primary income-producing activity? If so engaged for primary income, the expenses are allowed.

Schedule C : Deduction Categories		
Sequence	ITEM	Amount
001	Advertising (printing & promotions)	
002	Bad debts (accrual method only)	
003	Bank charges (include credit cards)	
004	Car & truck expenses (business only)	
005	Commissions (paid to others)	
006	Contract labor (nonemployees)	
007	Depreciation (from Form 4562)	
008	Dues & pubs. (seminars & newsletters)	
009	Employee benefits (food, prizes, & awards)	
010	Freight out (postage & parcel post)	
011	Insurance (business only)	
012	Interest: Mortgage (on business realty)	
013	Interest: Other (on business loans)	
014	Laundry & cleaning (include uniforms)	
015	Legal & professional (consultants)	
016	Office expense (stationery & other)	
017	Pension plans (for employees only)	
018	Rent (paid on business property)	
019	Repairs (painting & maintenance)	
020	Supplies (small tools & materials)	
021	Taxes (payroll, property, licenses)	
022	Travel & lodging (documented)	
023	Meals & entertainment (less 20% for yourself)	
024	Phone & utilities (business only)	
025	Wages (gross amount: nonshop)	
026 to 030	Other expenses (SPECIFY)	

Fig. 7.3 - Preprinted Deduction Lines on Schedule C (1040)

Subsection280A(c)(1) says that the disallowance rule—

shall not apply to any item to the extent such item is allocable to a portion of the dwelling unit which is exclusively used on a regular basis—
    *(A) as the **principal place** for any trade or business of the taxpayer,* [or]
    *(B) as a **place of business** which is used by patients, clients, or customers in meeting or dealing with the taxpayer in the normal course of his trade or business.*
The term "principal place" includes [that] *which is used . . . for administrative or management activities . . . if there is no other fixed location of such trade or business.*

The phrase "portion of the dwelling unit" means the business use portion or percentage (BUP). The BUP is determined by taking square footage measurements of the office space (including walls, access, and storage), and dividing this figure by the total living space (square footage) of the residence. A diagrammatic sketch of the office-in-home arrangement, with all dimensions thereon, becomes an important tax document.

There is also another requirement: "exclusive use" on a "regular basis." In other words, your office-in-home must have all the earmarks and similarities to a regular business office that you could have rented in a commercial complex. It has to be devoid of facilities for overnight family living. A toilet and coffee pot would be O.K., but go easy on TVs and DVDs. Once you have met this exclusivity requirement, you are entitled — proportionately — to such expenses as:

property taxes	telephone
mortgage interest	all utilities
hazard insurance	office supplies
painting & repairs	office equipment
cleaning & maintenance	carpets & drapes
depreciation	furniture & fixtures

That is, you are entitled to these expenses so long as you keep separate business records on them. You must go out of your way to avoid any commingling of these expenses with your personal and family living expenditures.

Car & Truck Expenses

Many proprietors have two vehicles that are used for business purposes. They have a passenger auto and a light truck or van. They may have other vehicles, but these two are typical. The car is used for calling on customers and suppliers, seminar attendance, appearance at government offices, and so on. The truck or van is used for pickup of supplies purchased and for delivery of products sold, for carrying tools and parts, for installation and repair services, and for the cartage of samples and catalogs.

Here, again, we run into the implication of personal and family use. To a tax agent, any use of a car or truck in a proprietorship business is deemed to be personally used, unless proven otherwise. This means that, unless a BUP (business use percentage) can be established convincingly, no expense for operating the vehicle is business allowed.

In the case of a passenger auto, the BUP proof requires maintaining a very detailed *mileage log*. This requires detailing your: (a) business miles, (b) commuting miles, (c) personal miles, and (d) total mileage for the year. Your BUP is mileage (a) divided by mileage (d). There is no use trying to rationalize or argue that your passenger auto is 100% used in business. It may well be. Even if you have a separate car for your personal use, and a separate car for the personal use of each of your family members, the IRS simply will not take your word for it. They want to see a mileage log showing dates, places, distances, and business purpose. If you have your office at home and a place of business elsewhere, you are commuting from home to work. This is nonbusiness use.

The situation is different with a truck or van that is fitted out for your particular business. If it has special racks, shelves, tie-down bars and hooks, and other modifications for hauling supplies, inventory, tools, and displays, you may be able to convince a tax agent that, indeed, you have a 100% business vehicle. This is especially convincing if you have a very uncomfortable nondriver's seat, and the vehicle is not suitable for weekend camping. To establish this, you should have complete photographs of the vehicle: front, back, side, and interior.

With proper attention to your business use needs, your truck or van may qualify as a *nonpersonal use vehicle*. This means a vehicle that, by reason of its nature, is not likely to be used more than a de minimis amount for personal purposes. If this is so, there is no mileage log requirement as per Sections 274(i) and 280F(d)(5)(B)(iii) of the tax code.

Once you have met the mileage log requirements for a passenger auto and the "qualified nonpersonal use" requirements for a truck or van, you are entitled to the following expense deductions . . . for each vehicle separately:

gas & oil	license fees
tires & batteries	parking & tolls
repairs	garaging costs
maintenance	car washes
insurance	installed items
interest payments	rental payments

Obviously, you must have records to substantiate the car and truck expenses that you enter on Schedule C.

Travel, Meals, & Entertainment

There is one tax subject that we are quite reluctant to touch on. It is a very sensitive expenditure category called TME (Travel, Meals, & Entertainment). Tax agents fancifully imagine that every struggling proprietorships is living high on the hog — wining and dining and living gloriously — at government expense. As a result of this unrestrained imagination by the IRS, very tough tax laws have been enacted to limit all TME expense deductions.

The IRS regulations on TME expenditures would fill this entire book. The key reference on point is Regulation 1.274: *Disallowance of Certain Entertainment, Gift, Travel, and Meal Expenses.* It consists of approximately 30,000 words. Yes: 30,000 words! If you prefer a shorter version, Code Section 274 (Disallowance of Certain Entertainment, Etc., Expenses) consists of approximately 5,000 words.

The term "travel" for tax purposes means *away from home overnight* . . . on a bona fide business trip. It includes transportation and lodging only. The term "meals" means any food or beverage, which is not lavish or extravagant, consumed when the taxpayer on business is present. The term "entertainment" means gifts and social affairs (theater, sport events, banquets, dancing) which have a clear business purpose.

Needless to say, every item of TME expenses must be documented in detail: Who, What, When, Where, and Why. Yet, even with the most painstaking records, only 50% of the meals and entertainment is deductible.

On Schedule C, your TME gets special treatment. There is a separate subschedule thereon that requires four line entries. We have enlarged and presented this subschedule in Figure 7.4. Any entry on a TME line over a few hundred dollars is guaranteed to be a picky-picky issue by the IRS. In the IRS's eyes, any TME expense entry is an abhorrent act by a taxpayer in business.

Other Expenses (Specify)

If you glance at Figures 7.2, 7.3, and 7.4 for a moment, you will note that the last deduction entry line is "Other expenses." You are instructed to specify these expenses in Part V. This means that you must identify, reference, and list the amount of each such expense. You cannot insert "miscellaneous" and enter whatever amount you want. For Schedule C purposes, there is no such thing as a miscellaneous expense. In your mind, some expense category may well be. But, if the category is $100 or more, itemize it out. If less than $100, add it to some analogous category as a "de minimis" item.

If you incur other types of business expenses that are not officially listed on page 1 of Schedule C or elsewhere in IRS regulations, you may enter them, as appropriate, on page 2 at "Other expenses." There are nine lines in Part V for this purpose. Each line space is about six inches long. This implies that you are expected to make each entry as self-explanatory as possible. Without your realizing it, this spacing is an opportunity to disclose any questionable deductions that, without disclosure and discovery by the IRS, could cost you dearly in negligence penalties.

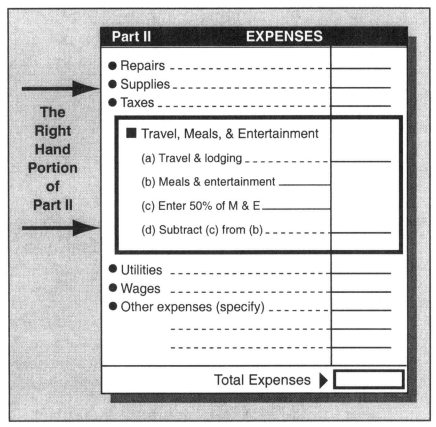

Fig. 7.4 - The TME Subschedule on Schedule C (1040)

All types of business expense deductions come under the general tax code Section 162: *Trade or Business Expenses*. The opening sentence reads in full as—

There shall be allowed as a deduction all the ordinary and necessary expenses paid or incurred during the taxable year in carrying on any trade or business.

This section is more commonly referred to as the "ordinary and necessary" (O&N) rule. Hence, if you have an O&N expense that is not line categorized on Schedule C, you enter it on the other expense line.

What are some examples of "other expenses"?

For one, Amortization. (It appears as Part VI on Form 4562.) There is no categorical line for this on Schedule C. So, enter it in the first blank space under other expenses as—

Amortization: Form 4562.............................. $_____

Another example: Suppose you incurred some research and experimental expenditures in connection with your business. This is a Section 174(a) deduction. You enter it on the next blank space with a short explanation as—

Sec. 174(a) expense: new product line............ $_____

A third example could be educational expenses for maintaining or improving your skills as an entrepreneur or specialist. A situation like this is covered by Regulation 1.162-5(c). On Schedule C, do not use the phrase "educational expenses"; it has prebusiness connotations. Instead, use "professional development" and enter on the third blank space as—

Prof. develop. Reg. 1.162-5(c) .... $_____

We are trying to stress an important point with these three examples. You give a short (acceptable sounding) description of the expense, and immediately follow it with a specific reference. The reference may be a tax form number, a code section, or a tax regulation number. For other allowable expenses, you may reference a Revenue Ruling or Tax Court decision. By citing specific references, you are putting the IRS on notice that you know what you are doing.

Proprietorship Pros and Cons

The primary advantage of a sole proprietorship is that it lends itself to a family operation. Husband, wife, and children can run the business with little outside help from others. All profits from the business accrue to the headmaster (or headmistress) of the family. The wife can be employed by the husband, or vice versa, and the children can be employed by either.

If the husband is the owner, he can employ his wife in the business. Whether he pays her wages or not depends on their working relationship, their handling of finances, and whether the wife wants a separate social security earnings record of her own.

If wages are paid to the wife, the husband is subject to all of the same employer taxes and withholdings of a giant corporation. (Recall Chapter 4). This means **two** social security/medicare taxes to pay: his and hers. The wife's social security/medicare tax is paid via Form W-2 procedures; the husband's social security/medicare tax is paid via Schedule SE (1040) as self-employment tax. If the spouses have been — or plan to be — married more than ten years (both under 65), the wife will get 50% of her husband's social security benefits . . . without his paying any wages to her. If both spouses are over age 65, the wife will get 100% of her husband's benefits (upon his demise) . . . without her being paid wages.

Wages paid to children employed by their parents are exempt from the social security tax. This exemption, however, applies only up to the age of 18. After this age, the parents must withhold the social security tax on all wages paid. In most cases, after — and often before — reaching age 18, the children no longer want to work for their parents. Meanwhile, they will have received valuable business training which can be helpful to them in the outside world.

There is one principal disadvantage to a proprietorship. If the tax owner becomes disabled or dies, the business generally goes downhill. Customers who like doing business with the husband and wife start drifting away. They go to other similar husband and wife businesses. In a compatible marriage, a husband and wife in business portray a certain "accommodating balance" towards their customers. This customer balance is difficult to maintain alone by the ongoing spouse.

By far the biggest advantage of self-employment is that one is not forced to retire at a specified age. When working for established companies, age 55 tends to be the critical point beyond which "forced retirement" becomes the norm. In some industries, age 60 is the force-out time. For everyone else, age 65 is it! You must retire; you have no choice.

Not so, when self-employed. Depending on your health and mental well-being, you can work to age 70, 75, 80, 85, 90 . . . or whatever. By doing so, you probably won't be making millions and millions of dollars, but you won't be bored with old age either. You'll live longer and be the envy of those who were force-retired to live on a shoestring.

For summary and check-list purposes, other advantages and disadvantages of a proprietorship are presented in Figure 7.5.

PROPRIETORSHIP			
ADVANTAGES		**DISADVANTAGES**	
1.	Simple one-man (or one woman) business; one owner; one decision maker (includes spouse).	1.	Financial resources limited; equity loan(s) on personal residence often needed.
2.	Can use own true name, followed by DBA (doing business as); register fictitious name(s) with county clerk.	2.	Many a 12-15 hour work day during peak season; if spouse nonactive, is difficult to get "substitute" manager.
3.	No written documentation required; can start, stop, change nature of business without giving official public notice.	3.	Lawsuits can endanger entire personal estate; wild allegations when no written contracts to be interpreted.
4.	Can operate out of own home or garage to cut overhead; business sign not needed if large address numbers displayable.	4.	Zoning ordinances may restrict "in home" businesses, if delivery trucks, auto parking, and walk-in traffic troublesome.
5.	Can employ own children, neighbors children, friends, & part-time "independent contractors".	5.	Teenagers and part-time help not always reliable; owner subject to penalties if part-timers seek unemployment & social security benefits.
6.	Net profits of the business shared with no one but the owner (and his/her spouse).	6.	Net earnings potential rather limited; other than certain "high end" professions, rarely can net earnings exceed $100,000.

Fig. 7.5 - Other Pros and Cons of a Proprietorship

8

PARTNERSHIP: FORM 1065

A Partnership Is Not A Taxable Entity. As Such, Its Form 1065 Is An "Information" Return: Not A Tax Return. It Consists Of Income Sources, Allowable Deductions, Cost Of Goods, Balance Sheets, And Data On The Participation Of Partners. The 1065 Information Is Distributively Allocated And "Passed Through" To Each Partner. Ideally, The Partnership Accounting Year Should End On September 30. This Allows 90 Days Before Each Partner Closes His Tax Books On December 31. Each Partner's "Distributive Share" Is Itemized On A Schedule K-1 (1065) Which Directs Attention To Specific Tax Forms Each Partner Must Use.

In this chapter we address partnerships, their tax forms, and their peculiarities of tax treatment. As you will soon see, a partnership return is significantly more complex than a proprietorship return. Part of this is due to the fact that more than one owner is involved. Although many of the profit/loss elements are the same, there are other elements in a partnership return that are not present in a proprietorship.

The basic partnership return is Form 1065. This form is officially titled: *U.S. Return of Partnership Income*. Compare this with Form 1040 which is titled: *U.S. Individual Income Tax Return*. Note the titling difference. The partnership form uses the phrase "Return of Income," whereas the proprietorship form uses "Income Tax Return." What is missing in the Form 1065 title?

The word "**tax**" does not appear.

A partnership, in and of itself, is not a taxable entity. Yes: a tax accountable income or loss is determined. Whatever the amount is, it is passed through — proportionately — to the individual partners for taxing on each of their own separate Forms 1040. There is no tax computation whatsoever on a partnership return. More appropriately, then, a partnership 1065 is an *information* return, rather than a tax return.

A partnership can consist of any two or more persons (3, 10, 50) who join together to carry on a trade or business. If there are too many persons involved, matters can get overly complex. This is because the tax information from Form 1065 has to be equitably reconciled, before being passed through to each partner.

Since this is an instructional guide, we want to avoid unnecessary complications. For our purposes, therefore, we will consider a partnership as consisting of three unrelated persons, each of whom is a "material participant" in the new business. They work together for livelihood purposes, rather than for tax shelter benefits. This is the essence of a *general partnership* in which each partner is allocably liable for his own misdeeds, and co-liable for the misdeeds of his partners. The accounting principles are the same whether for 10 or more general partners.

The Partnership Accounting Year

One of the first acts of reconciliation is for the partners-to-be to adopt an allowable accounting year for the partnership. This is important because the partnership is an entity separate and apart from the individual partners themselves. As a separate accounting entity, a separate set of books is required. Posting, maintaining, and summarizing the accounts at a specific year-end date is absolutely essential to the success of the partnership.

For a newly formed partnership, the general rule is that the partnership year must end . . . *within or with the taxable year of the partner(s)* [Sec. 706(a)]. Most individual partners are on a calendar year basis. It is a rare exception to be otherwise. Hence, the phrase "within or with" means before or on December 31.

If, in a three-member partnership, the partnership year also ends on December 31, that becomes four tax returns to be simultaneously reconciled. This is the seedbed for making mistakes and for causing arguments and disharmony between partners. Tax return preparation is an acid test of self-discipline and resolve. Not all Form 1040 filers function with the same degree of conscientiousness. Now you know why we are limiting our discussion to three-person partnerships. The more the number of general partners, the more the accounting bickerings.

To avoid the December 31 accounting panic, we urge adopting a partnership year ending on September 30. This is the end of a calendar quarter: the 3rd quarter. A calendar quarter accounting year coincides nicely with employer quarterly returns and quarterly sales/use tax returns. A September 30 partnership year precedes each partner's calendar year by 90 days. This should be ample time to get the partnership books in order, and pass the results on through to the individual partners.

Unfortunately, the partners cannot arbitrarily adopt a September 30 partnership year on their own. They must obtain IRS approval. This requires filing Form 1128: *Application to Adopt, Change, or Retain a Tax Year*, and stating the reasons for wanting September 30. Section 706(b)(1)(c) authorizes the IRS to insist on a *business purpose* for any date other than December 31.

If the nature of the partnership business is such that there is a "natural business year," you have a legitimate reason for change. Most businesses have natural peak and nonpeak periods. If you have such a natural business year, do claim it.

In most cases, the IRS will approve Form 1128 if the partnership date requested is not earlier than September 30 or not later than December 31. Other than this 90-day "window," approval for other partnership accounting years can be obtained. But it is difficult. The partnership has to have at least three years of prior operating experience in order to deviate from the September 30-December 31 window.

Written Partnership Agreement

A partnership is an unincorporated combination of persons of legal age who agree, formally or informally — orally or in writing — to conduct a business jointly. There must be a mutual intent and desire to so join. There also must be a mutual desire to actually conduct a valid business for profit-seeking purposes. Each partner thereto must devote his "best efforts" towards achieving the partnership goal. In addition, each partner must contribute money, property, or services (or a combination thereof).

If one contributes money, property, and/or services to a business venture, some common sense should prevail. Foremost in this regard is that the partnership agreement be in writing. It need not be a formal document with high-sounding legalese. Just something in writing, logically organized, and in words and phrases that all partners understand. All partners should read and sign the agreement in the presence of at least one witness, preferably a Notary Public. Does this not make good sense?

All partnerships have one bad feature. They start falling apart when the first ill winds of business blow. In the euphoria of creation, everyone agrees amicably to share in the profits. Everyone also has an obligation to share in the losses and setbacks. If a squeamish partner starts turning away, you want a contractual document to hold his feet to the fire. In short, you want a legally enforceable contract. This means that the partnership agreement must be in writing and signed by all parties concerned. Do not commit your money, property, or time until you have a meaningful partnership agreement in hand.

While profit and loss sharing is a requisite of any partnership, the profits and losses need not be shared in exact proportion to the value of each partner's contributed capital, property, or services. So long as the nonproportionate sharing is spelled out in the partnership agreement, the IRS generally will accept the agreed-to allocations. There is only one condition that the IRS imposes on non-proportionate sharing. That is, the economic reasoning for the nonproportionate sharing must be sound, and it must be independent of obvious tax benefits to prosperous partners.

Some of the introductory points of a sound but simple partnership agreement are presented in Figure 8.1. Some partnership agreements can run 10 to 15 pages. This is much too long. It is impossible to cover every potentially unforeseen contingency. Three pages covering the high points are enough. Do note, particularly, in Figure 8.1 that a *managing partner* is designated. This is the person responsible for all recordkeeping and tax accounting for the partnership. His/her primary qualification is the ability to schedule timely tax forms completion.

PARTNERSHIP AGREEMENT

This AGREEMENT is made between

_____ , (called Partner "A")
_____ , (called Partner "B")
and _____ , (called Partner "C")

These parties voluntarily associate themselves together as General Partners for the purpose of conducting the business of _____
_____
_____ .

Name & Duration: The name of the partnership shall be ____
_____. The partnership shall continue until dissolved by mutual consent or as otherwise terminated.

Place of Business: The principal place of business shall be
_____ and such other place or places as may be mutually agreed upon.

Initial Capital: The initial capital of the partnership shall be
$_____ , and each partner shall contribute as follows:

Partner "A"	$_____	*(or the equivalent)*
Partner "B"	$_____	*(or the equivalent)*
Partner "C"	$_____	*(or the equivalent)*

Books of Account: The partnership shall keep accurate, up-to-date, and complete books of account at all times. Said books shall be open to examination by any partner.

Managing Partner: The partners mutually agree that _____
_____ (Partner "A") shall act as managing partner to prepare the books of account, all tax returns, and all other documents pertaining to the business.

WITNESSED BY

Notary Public

_____

_____

Executed at _____ on _____

_____ , Partner "A"
_____ , Partner "B"
_____ , Partner "C"

Fig. 8.1 - Introductory Points in a Partnership Agreement

A partnership is presumed to be ongoing and continuing from year to year, unless it is terminated. Section 708(b) spells out when termination occurs. In part, this tax code section reads—

A partnership shall be considered as terminated only if—
   (A)   no part of any business, financial operation, or venture of the partnership continues to be carried on by any of its partners . . . or,
   (B)   within a 12-month period there is a sale or exchange of 50 percent or more of the total interest in the partnership capital and profits.

Although it is not necessary to put this termination rule in the partnership agreement, it is a good idea to do so. It may save misunderstandings when a more than 50% partner (or partners) withdraws from the activity.

Each Partner's Capital Account

One of the first accounting tasks for the managing partner is to set up a separate capital account for each partner. This can be done on a single ledger with separate columns assigned to each partner. The capital accounts are used for determining each partner's proportionate ownership interest in the partnership, and for allocating his distributive share items at the end of each partnership accounting year.

If each partner contributed money only — and nothing else — each partner's beginning capital account would be quite simple. Money in cash or check is denoted in dollars. Thus, the capital account of each of three partners would be—

Partner A   —   X dollars
Partner B   —   Y dollars
Partner C   —   Z dollars

Most active partnerships, however, are formed largely with property and services being contributed. There is some money contributed but, often, the amount is less than 50% of the initial capitalization of the venture. Property is contributed in the form of real estate, machinery and equipment, materials and supplies, inventory, accounts receivable, securities, installment notes, and so on. Services are contributed in the form of past services rendered, special expertise and know-how, and the guaranteed immediate performance of services without pay.

All nonmonetary contributions have to be fair market valued at the time of their acceptance by the partnership. Written appraisals and other estimates and documentation are needed to back up the dollar value assigned to each contributor. Special rules apply (Sec. 724) for unrealized receivables, inventory items, and capital loss property. When all property and services are fair valued, they are treated thereafter as ordinary capital.

Each partner's capital account has a "beginning of year" and an "end of year" amount. In between these two amounts, various changes take place. There may be additional capital contributions or capital withdrawals. There are allocations of ordinary income or loss, capital gain or loss, nontaxable income, unallowable losses, and other internal accounting adjustments (for loans, bad debts, credits, and other items).

A sample capital account ledger for a three-person partnership is presented in Figure 8.2. For each entry line, there is a separate account for each partner, and a summary total for all partners. Entry lines (d) and (e) particularly should be noted. These are transactional items that do not show up directly in the income/loss accounting for the partnership. They are separate distributive pass-throughs. Imagine having 50 partners!

There is one other line entry to note in Figure 8.2. It is line (h): *partner-days*. In some business ventures, the number of partners comes and goes. They "buy in" and "sell out" on short notice. When they do, the partnership mix is changed from that of the initial formation. To properly allocate the distributive share items, the capital-active number of days of each partner in the partnership year should be recorded.

Quick Overview of Form 1065

The partnership Form 1065 is significantly more complex than the proprietorship Schedule C (1040). There are several reasons for this. The principal reason is that in a partnership there are more owners and more capital available to engage in a multiplicity of ventures, simultaneously. There are portfolio income and expenses, rental real estate income and expenses, capital gains and losses, and investments in other partnerships and businesses. There is also a balance sheet requirement for identifying the assets and liabilities of the partnership.

	CAPITAL ITEM	Partner "A"	Partner "B"	Partner "C"	TOTAL (All Partners)
(a)	Beginning of year				
(b)	Contributed during year				
(c)	Ordinary income (loss)				
(d)	Income not in (c)	Capital gain & return / Nontaxable interest / Other (see instructions)			
(e)	Losses not in (c)	Capital losses / Nondeductible expenses / Other (see instructions)			
(f)	Withdrawals & distributions				
(g)	End of year				
(h)	Partner days				▼ ▼ Sch. M-2 Form 1065

Fig. 8.2 - Capital Account Ledger for Each Individual Partner

With these preliminary comments in mind, it is instructive to present a quick overview of the format-content of Form 1065. We do this in Figure 8.3. Note that we show two "spread sheets"; but actually, Form 1065 consists of *four* full pages. We have taken much liberty to simplify Form 1065 for purposes here.

At the top of page 1 of Form 1065, there are separate entry spaces for date business started, and for total assets at end of year.

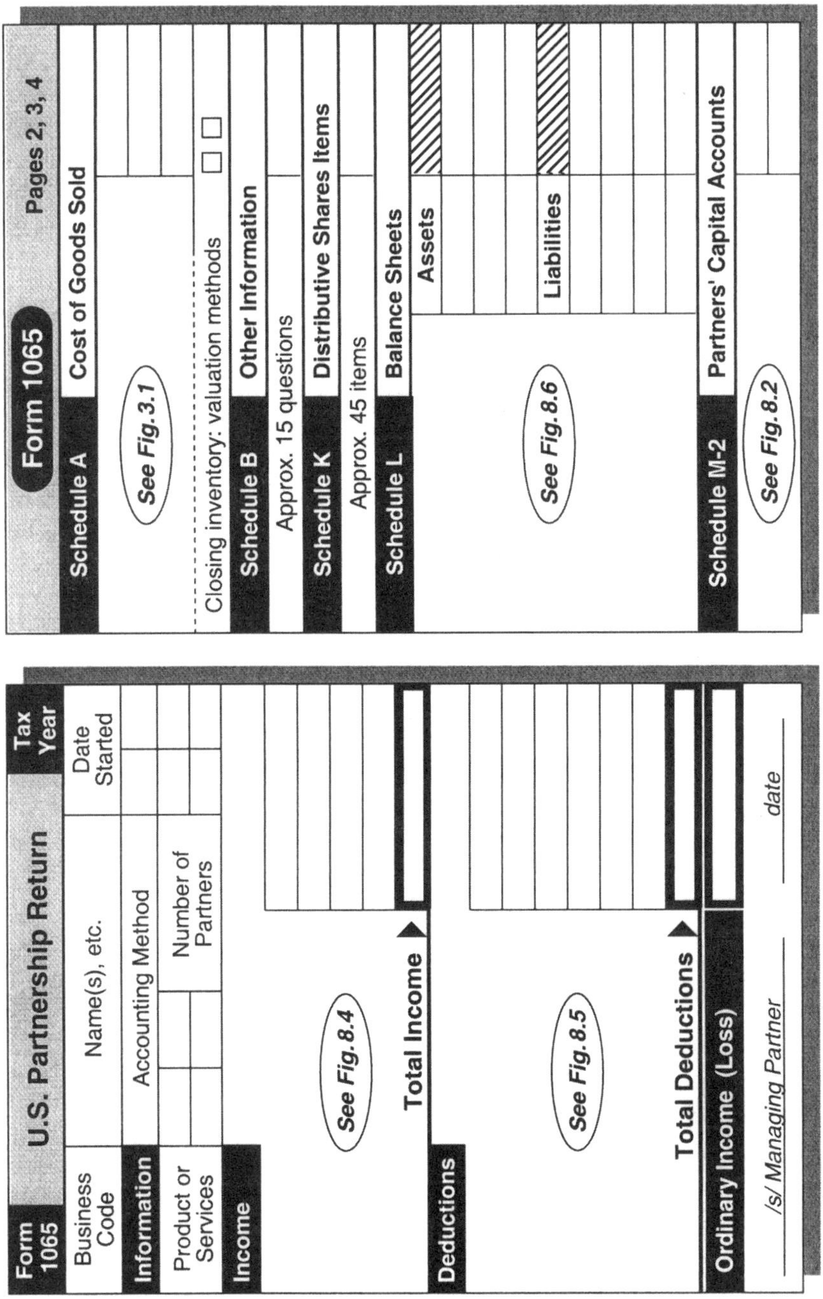

Fig. 8.3 - Oversimplified Format / Contents of Partnership Return of Income

There also are a number of checkboxes that focus on the type of return, method of accounting, and number of partners in the partnership. For each partner, "distributive sharing" is required.

The income and deductions portions of page 1 are comparable — somewhat — to the profit or loss format-content of a proprietorship. But more items and more segregations are required. The bottom line on Form 1065 is officially designated *Ordinary income (loss)* rather than net profit or loss. This is because there is no netting until the partnership pass-throughs are combined with each partner's other sources of income.

Pages 2, 3, and 4 of Form 1065 consist of five schedules as identified in Figure 8.3. **Schedule A** (Cost of Goods Sold) has been covered previously in Chapter 3 (Figure 3.1). There are a few more questions on the valuing of closing inventory, especially with regard to "subnormal" goods and "full absorption" of manufacturing costs. Partnerships tend to be suspect of tax gamesmanship, and so more questions and checkboxes are used.

Schedule B (Other Information) asks some 12 to 15 questions in Yes-No checkbox form. These focus on the type of partnership, whether other partnerships are involved, and whether there are any foreign partners. Questions are also asked as to whether the partnership is publicly traded, whether it is a tax shelter, and whether there are any foreign bank accounts. If there were any distributions from the partnership by sale or death during the year, an attached statement is required showing basis adjustments to the remaining partners. At the very end of Schedule B, there is a separate space for *Designation of Tax Matters Partner* (the Managing partner).

Schedule K (Distributive Share Items) lists approximately 45 different items of income, deductions, and credits that are allocated to each partner individually. For this allocation, an associated Schedule **K-1** (1065) is required.

Schedule L (Balance Sheets) consists of some 20 asset and liability entry lines. Schedule L is required when the gross receipts of the partnership exceed $250,000, or its total assets exceed $600,000. Directly below Schedule L, there is a Schedule M-1 (Reconciliation of Books with Return) and a Schedule M-2 (Partners' Capital Accounts). We have already introduced you to Schedule M-2 in Figure 8.2.

We meant it when we said a "quick overview" of Form 1065. We just wanted to introductively familiarize you with it. As you can sense, it is not an ordinary profit or loss statement.

Multiple Sources of Income

Unlike a proprietorship that focuses primarily on one trade or business, with some incidental other income source, a partnership can conduct several primary businesses simultaneously. Much depends on the individual expertise of the individual partners. Usually, there is one primary (core) business in which all partners materially participate. Then there are one or more satellite businesses, each overseen and managed by a separate partner. There can be rental income property, participation in a farming or mining venture, affiliation with another partnership, investments in mutual funds, and so on.

To accommodate the multiplicity of income sources, the income portion of Form 1065 has to be expanded significantly. For each separate income source, a separate backup schedule is needed. This is for tracking purposes. All income into the partnership is not treated the same when passed through to the individual partners. For example, material participation income is subject to social security tax, whereas rental income, capital gain income, and interest/dividend income are not subject to said tax. Certain items, such as rental income and portfolio income, are subject to passive loss and interest expense limitation rules. Tracing all income sources, therefore, becomes particularly important for pass-through designation purposes.

In Figure 8.4, we present an edited and rearranged version of the income portion of Form 1065 (page 1). Note that lines 1 through 5 represent the "core business" of the partnership; lines 6 through 14 are the "satellite" businesses.

Deductions Sequence Rearranged

All businesses are entitled to certain current expense deductions. We presented a rather extensive list of these deductions (for a proprietorship) in Figure 7.3. Similar deductions apply to a partnership. The difference is the sequence of arrangement. Certain deductions are prioritized in a partnership for pass-through reasons and for highlighting terms of the partnership agreement.

Page 1	PARTNERSHIP INCOME		TAX YEAR
No.	ITEM		Amount
1	Gross receipts or sales		/////
2	LESS returns & allowances		/////
3	Balance (adjusted gross receipts)		
4	Cost of goods sold		
5	Gross profit (subtract line 4 from line 3)		
6	Income (loss) from other partnerships		
7	Income (loss) from fiduciaries		
8	Portfolio income (loss)		/////
9	Rental realty income (loss)		/////
10	Other rental income (loss)	[Equip. rental]	
11	Net royalty income (loss)	[Oil & gas]	
12	Net farm income (loss)	[Sch.F (1040)]	
13	Net form 4797 gain (loss)	[Asset sales]	
14	Other income (loss)	[Attach Sched.]	
/////		TOTAL INCOME ▶▶▶	

Fig. 8.4 - Rearranged Income Lines on Form 1065

For example, guaranteed payments to a partner or partners. Guaranteed payments are of two kinds: (1) compensation for services rendered by certain partners, and (2) interest on separate money temporarily loaned to the partnership by other partners.

A partner, as such, is not an employee of his partnership. This is because he is a part owner of the business and shares directly in its net profits. If he is to be assigned any compensation for his services, the assignment must be specifically set forth in the partnership agreement. If it is so, then his compensation is a "guaranteed payment." When properly documented, it is deductible from the partnership income.

A partner also is a venture capitalist. He has to advance (contribute) money to the partnership to get it started and keep it going. Ordinarily, a partner is not expected to lend money to his own partnership. He may do so, however, if sanctioned by the partnership agreement. Any loan by a partner to the partnership must be backed up with a promissory note signed by the partners, with the market rate of interest stated thereon. With this documentation, the interest paid to the partner is a guaranteed payment of the partnership, and deductible by it.

With the foregoing in mind, the sequence of deductions against the income of a partnership is presented in Figure 8.5. Do note the second deduction entry: *Salaries and wages*. These are *other than* any guaranteed payments to the partners, and other than direct labor in the cost-of-goods-sold schedule (Schedule A of Figure 8.3). The non-Schedule A deduction comprises the usual administrative salaries and wages paid to employees of the partnership. Whereas guaranteed payments may pass through as self-employment income, Form W-2 wages do not.

Also note the third deduction in Figure 8.5: Rent paid. Because a partnership has to have a central place of business, the renting of commercial office or shop space is quite typical. The location should coincide with the business address in the partnership agreement. If also sanctioned in the agreement, the partnership may rent tools, machinery, equipment, furniture, and fixtures. All rents paid for the business use of property is deductible. This does *not* include car rentals of any kind. Special disallowance rules apply to passenger vehicles valued at more than $15,000 [Section 280F].

Altogether there are about 12 preprinted deduction lines on Form 1065. This compares with approximately 25 for a proprietorship. The unlisted deductions on Form 1065 are all combined in the last entry: *Other deductions (attach schedule).* Make absolutely sure that none of the other deductions includes any personal expenditures of the partners, nor any losses on self-dealing transactions between the partners and the partnership.

Importance of Balance Sheets

Very few partnerships are all liquid: with nothing but cash money on hand or in the bank. There are certain tangible and intangible assets that are carried on the books from year to year. And there are certain legal obligations that remain to be paid.

Page 1	INCOME (Fig. 8.4)	TAX YEAR
	PARTNERSHIP DEDUCTIONS	

No.	ITEM	Amount
1	Guaranteed payments (to partners)	
2	Salaries & wages (not to partners)	
3	Rent paid (for buildings, equip., etc.)	
4	Deductible interest (core business only)	
5	Taxes, licenses, & permits	
6	Bad debts (accrual only)	
7	Repairs (to business property)	
8	Depreciation (from Form 4562)	
9	Amortization (from Form 4562)	
10	Retirement plans (employees only)	
11	Employee benefit programs	
12	Other deductions (attach schedule)	
	TOTAL DEDUCTIONS ▶ ▶ ▶	

Fig. 8.5 - Rearranged Deduction Lines on Form 1065

All assets and all liabilities of the partnership at the end of each accounting year are set forth on *balance sheets*. The plural "s" derives from the fact that there is a balance sheet for the beginning of the year, and another balance sheet at the end of the year. When placed side by side, the two balance sheets give a concise picture of the comparative asset holdings for that year.

Technically, the posting of balance sheets is not required unless the gross receipts of the partnership exceed $250,000, or its total assets exceed $600,000. But, as a partner, you want the information posted regardless of any tax requirement. This posting should be mandated in the partnership agreement. There is no better way of determining the "net worth" of a business than the posting of balance sheets. If done correctly, the net worth should exactly equal the combined capital accounts of all the partners. Hence, the balance sheets are a means for cross-checking and reconciling the *capital accounting* practices of the partnership.

Our edited version of the balance sheets for a partnership is presented in Figure 8.6.

Page 4	SCHEDULE L (FORM 1065)				TAX YEAR
		Beginning of year		End of year	
Assets		(a)	(b)	(c)	(d)
1	Cash & bank balances				
2	Accounts receivable				
	LESS uncollectibles				
3	Inventories				
4	Notes & bonds				
5	Other current assets				
6	Real estate loans				
7	Other investments				
8	Depreciable assets				
	LESS prior taken				
9	Depletable assets				
	LESS prior taken				
10	Land (at cost)				
11	Amortizable assets				
	LESS prior taken				
12	Other assets				
13	**TOTAL ASSETS**				
Liabilities & Partners' Capital					
14	Accounts payable				
15	Notes payable < 1 yr				
16	Other liabilities <1 yr				
17	Nonrecourse loans				
18	Notes payable > 1 yr				
19	Other liabilities				
20	PARTNERS' CAPITAL				
21	**TOTAL Liabilities**				

Fig. 8.6 - Edited Contents of Partnership Balance Sheets

Actually, the categories listed, and the sequence shown, follow very closely the official format of Form 1065. We have tried to make the itemizations a little more self-explanatory. The "beginning of year" balance sheet is the "end of year" data from the preceding year.

Note in Figure 8.6 that the accounts receivable are reduced by the uncollectible accounts at the end of the year. Uncollectibles are those customer billings that are more than 90 days past due and for which a "final demand" in writing has been made. If there is no response of any kind within 30 days of the final demand, you might as well write the amounts off. Legal action for collection can be costly and is often ineffectual. Every partner should know the uncollectibles (bad debt) experience of his partnership.

The asset entries for depreciation, depletion, and amortization require subtractions of the accumulated deductions previously taken. This includes the current year's deduction as well. The net depreciation, net depletion, and net amortization are the "book value" of these assets at the end of the year. Unless there is a real estate involved, it is unlikely that any of these assets will appreciate in value with time. Hence, book value is a realistic tool for ascertaining the net worth of a business.

The liabilities of a business are valued in terms of time. Accounts that are due and payable within one year are classed as "current" items. Those that are due and payable in one year or more are classed as "long term." Most long-term accounts (be they assets or liabilities) run some risk of default. Attentive partners who take the time to examine the balance sheets will inquire into those risks and want some documented explanation.

Introduction to Schedule K-1

All of the foregoing has dealt with the features and preparation of Form 1065: U.S. Return of Partnership Income. Many of these features are identical (or nearly so) to those of LLCs and S corporations. This is why we spent a little extra time on developing the features. In the same sense that a partnership is a pass-through entity, so, too, are an LLC (in Chapter 9) and an S corporation (in Chapter 10). How is the entity information passed through to its participants?

Answer: via **Schedule K-1**. For a partnership, the Schedule K-1 (Form 1065) is titled: ***Partner's Share of Income, Deductions, Credits, Etc.***

The K-1 (1065) is a separate intermediate form of its own. It is "intermediate" between Form 1065 and Form 1040 for each partner. It is a summary of the distributive share of tax information derived from Form 1065 that is intended for Form 1040. It is accompanied by approximately 16,000 words of official instructions and tax code references.

Among other things, the instructions state that—

The purpose of Schedule K-1 is to report to you your share of the partnership's income, deductions, credits, etc. **Please keep it for your records. Do not file with your tax return.** *A copy has been filed with the IRS. . . . You are liable for your share of the partnership's income, whether or not distributed, and you must include your share on your tax return.*

Schedule K-1 is a very comprehensive tax document. It is prepared by the tax matters partner upon closing the books for each accounting year of the partnership. It is entirely too complex for a discussion of its preparation here. We only want to acquaint you with its features. This we do in an abbreviated version of its format and contents in Figure 8.7. Note that Figure 8.7 consists of approximately 50 entry items, and approximately 15 other associated tax forms. It actually covers two full pages (front and back), but we show only one.

Now you know why we urged earlier that the partnership adopt an accounting year that ends on September 30. The tax matters partner — and his bookkeeper/accountant — need adequate time to compile all the data and make the proper distributive share calculations. This allows 90 days before each partner has to close his own tax books on December 31.

There is a separate Schedule K-1 for each partner. Each K-1 displays each partner's name, address, and (of course) social security number, or EIN if an entity. At the bottom left-hand side on the front page, there is a subschedule: *Analysis of Partner's Capital Account.* This is a summary of each partner's capital participation in the business. This summary is where the Tax Matters Partner (TMP) has to reconcile and balance, collectively, all partners' end-of-year capital. You should review carefully your capital account entries, as well as all other entries on the K-1.

Sch. K-1 Form 1065	PARTNER'S DISTRIBUTIVE SHARE ITEMS		TAX YEAR
Partner's Soc. Sec. No.		Partnership's Fed. I.D. No.	
Name & address of partner		Name & address of partnership	
Questions, liabilities, & checkboxes ☐ ☐		Questions, percentages, & checkboxes ☐ ☐	
Partner's Capital Account			

Pass-through Item	Amount	Forms
Income (Loss) 8 items		Sch. B (1040) Sch. D (1040) Sch. E (1040) Form 4797
Deductions 4 items		Form 8283 Sch. A (1040)
Credits 6 items		Form 3468 Form 5884 Form 8586
Self-Employment 3 items		Sch. SE (1040)
Tax Preferences 6 items		Form 6251
Investment Interest 3 items		Form 4952
Foreign Taxes 5 items		Form 1116
Investment Credit Recapture 5 items		Form 4255
Other Items & Elections as provided by partnership		Form 4136 Form 8271 Form 8275 Form 8308

Fig. 8.7 - Abbreviated Contents of Schedule K-1 (Form 1065)

If you feel that an error has been made on your K-1, you should contact the tax matters partner. Often, what is believed to be an error is a misunderstanding of how partnership accounting works. It is different — and more complex — than your own individual tax accounting. This is because of the distributive share computations, the pass-through features, and the balance sheet requirements. If you have a negative end-of-year capital account, you pay tax on money you may never see. It was consumed *in* the partnership . . . to which you agreed. The partnership agreement must provide that you restore your negative balance to at least zero . . . preferably positive. Otherwise, you can lose your participation rights as a partner and/or be subject to lawsuit by the partnership. A partnership, as an entity, can sue its individual members.

Figuring Each "Distributive Share"

The determination of each partner's tax liability is set forth in Sections 701 through 709 of the tax code. These nine sections comprise over 400 *pages* of text! Of particular interest to us at this point is Section 704: *Partner's Distributive Share*. Subsection (a): *Effect of Partnership Agreement*, reads—

A partner's distributive share of income, gain, loss, deduction, or credit shall, except as otherwise provided . . ., be determined by the partnership agreement.

If the partnership agreement does not address distributive share items, then . . . *the partner's economic interest in the partnership . . . shall be determinative.*

One's "economic interest" in a partnership depends on two factors: (a) each partner's capital account, and (b) each partner's *participating days* in the partnership year. A partner who has risked his capital for 365 days is deserving of a larger distributive share than a partner who has risked his capital for, say, 100 days.

Let us illustrate the distributive share allocation with specific numbers. Consider the following:

	Capital at risk	Participating days
Partner A	$10,000	250
Partner B	10,000	365
Partner C	18,000	100

The distributive share percentage of any allocable item based on each partner's participating interest is as follows:

Partner A: $10,000 x 250/365 (0.6849) = $ 6,849 = 31.45%

Partner B: 10,000 x 365/365 (1.0000) = 10,000 = 45.92%

Partner C: 18,000 x 100/365 (0.2739) = 4,930 = 22.63%

$38,000 $21,779   100.00%

Whereas the total capital account for all partners is $38,000, the at-risk participating amount is $21,779. Of this amount, partner B's participating interest — for distributive share purposes — is $10,000 ÷ 21,779 or 45.92%. His ownership of capital, however, is $10,000 ÷ 38,000 or 26.31%.

Summary of Pros and Cons

The mixture of partner contributions to the business can be any arrangement agreed to between the persons involved. The agreement preferably should be in writing, and be signed by all partners. The partners can share equally or unequally in the profits and losses, so long as there is an enforceable contract under local law. This provides great flexibility to the business to meet changing economic conditions. Although the partners may share unequally in the "bottom line," they generally share (more or less) equally in the management of the business. This encourages balance, foresight, and compromise that are essential to success in any business, regardless of type.

Once formed in writing, a partnership becomes an *entity* separate and apart from its individual members. Within this entity, a separate "capital account" for each partner is maintained. Thus, each partner can add to, or withdraw from, his own capital account. The conditions for doing so usually are set forth in the partnership agreement. Contributions and withdrawals will change the ownership mix of the entity with the passing of time.

The main disadvantage of a general partnership is that each member is personally liable for all debts of the entity, should other members fail to live up to their agreement. This is called "joint and several liability." Many a conscientious partner has been stuck with all the business debts — including taxes — of his associates, long after a partnership has broken up. Partnerships tend to break up rapidly when there are downturns in business.

PARTNERSHIP		
ADVANTAGES		**DISADVANTAGES**
1.	Near ideal for 3-5 principals whose individual talents comple- ment each other; co-equality in management decisions.	1.	If one or more partners start "slacking off' or "overdraw" their capital accounts, serious bicker- ing and mistrust occur.
2.	Written "partnership agreement" can be prepared without ratifica- tion by government agency; all parties co-sign in presence of each other.	2.	Initial agreement is seldom up- dated, amended, or modified as relationships in business unfold; reality enters and lawsuits often follow.
3.	More resources available; part- ners can contribute any mix of money, property, skill, & labor for which agreed values can be assigned.	3.	Where other than money is con- tributed, "capital accounting" poses severe problems when non-monetary contributors seek "draw down" of their accounts.
4.	Principal place of business can be rented in commercial area & paid secretary hired; partners can work out of their own home(s) using their own car(s).	4.	Commercial space rental often requires long-term leases with penalties for premature termin- ation; workers "play" when the boss is away.
5.	Business property such as mach- inery, equipment, furniture, fix- tures, leases, franchises, coven- ants have "pass-through" bene- fits to individual partners.	5.	Because of the diversity of indi- vidual partner interests, accurate & stringent recordkeeping is re- quired; poor records invite intra- partner controversies.
6.	Can avoid permanent employees by hiring a "temporary service" agency to supply workers as needed; maximizes pension & profit sharing benefits to partners	6.	Workers with families seek in- come security with fringe bene- fits; they accept temporary em- ployment as "last resort"; they tend to be unhappy... always looking elsewhere.

Fig. 8.8 - Other Pros and Cons of a Partnership

Another disadvantage of partnerships is spousal interferences. Partnership accounting rules and taxation matters are quite different from ordinary wage earner situations. Oftentimes, a partner has to pay income tax on money that he does not actually receive. Some taxable money has to stay in the business to keep operations going, pay employees, buy inventory, get new equipment, maintain lines of credit, and so on. For spouses who are not active in the business themselves, this is difficult to understand. Such spouses also view their partner's capital account as another (federally insured) depository account which can be withdrawn — or borrowed against — at will. The minute that a partner's spouse or other family member begins making financial demands on the partnership, trouble brews. Inevitably, bickering among the partners grows, and soon the business fails.

For summary and check-list purposes, other advantages and disadvantages of a partnership are presented in Figure 8.8. A well-structured partnership can go beyond the disability or death of any one partner. This is because a *partnership interest* — as determined by each partner's capital account — is a capital asset. It can be sold or transferred to another person in the private domain, or it can be bought out by other partners.

9

LIMITED LIABILITY COMPANY

The "LL" In LLC Is A Misleading - Though Exciting - Premise. After Registering ARTICLES OF ORGANI- ZATION In One's Home State, The Granting Of LLC Status Does Not Invalidate Contractual Obligations To Customers, Clients, Vendors, Suppliers, And Employees. Cash Starving A Business And Walking Away When Debts And Claims Start Piling Up, Destroys All LLC Protections. Such Protections Apply Only To Frivolous-Type Lawsuits Against The Personal Assets Of A Targeted Member. An OPERATING AGREEMENT, Books Of Account, And "Mandatory" Make-up Capital Are Required. All Business Obligations Must Be Paid!

An LLC — Limited Liability Company — is an unincorporated business entity. That is, it is an "entity" so long as its members maintain a set of books of account (income and expenses; assets and liabilities) that are separate and apart from the recordkeeping requirements of the individual members themselves. It is on this premise that all 50 U.S. states (and the District of Columbia) have enacted separate LLC laws of their own. The result is that an LLC is a special entity created under *state law*: **not** under federal law.

In the broader sense, an LLC is a hybrid entity. It has the managerial flexibility of a proprietorship, the profit and loss pass-through features of a partnership, and the limited liability trump card of a corporation. Unlike a corporation, though, an LLC does not enjoy indefinite life. State law conditions prevail.

The attractiveness of an LLC as a form of business lies in its two letters "LL": Limited Liability. For years, the fear in the heart of every owner of a small business has been the potential of a lawsuit. In such a litigious society as the United States, there is always some perceived wrongdoing by the business itself, or some alleged misconduct by an owner, manager, employee, or agent thereof. Most small businesses barely keep enough capital on hand to meet their operating needs. Because so, the primary target for lawsuit is the personal assets of the principals of the business: their homes, bank accounts, investments, realty holdings, and future earnings. To limit frivolous lawsuits, there is some protection under each state's LLC statute.

The feature of "limited liability" does not bestow upon an LLC a free-wheeling, responsibility-avoiding arrangement for exploitative entrepreneurship. The painful reality is that there are articles of organization to be filed with state authorities and fees to be paid; there are operating agreements to be worked out; there is a minimum capital base to be maintained; there are books and records to be kept; there are balance sheets to be balanced; there are tax returns to be filed; and there are contracts with customers, creditors, and suppliers to be honored. In the end, every LLC has to take its place in line demonstrating responsible behavior, as do other entities, both corporate and noncorporate.

Forming an LLC

Unlike a sole proprietorship or a general partnership, the formation of an LLC is a legal process under state law. The logical question arises: Under which state law? It is that state within which the LLC's principal place of business is intended to be conducted. Once formed in one state, a domestic LLC is reciprocally recognized in other states for legal and business purposes. Some states, California is one example, recognize a single-member LLC but many states do not. The IRS does not recognize a single-member LLC. You should be aware of this fact, should you start an LLC with two members and, subsequently, one member drops out.

To really get started, you need to contact the Secretary of State in which you intend to do business. Direct your inquiries to that state's *Limited Liability Company Unit*. Ask about applicable forms, instructions, and fees. All you really want to know, initially, are the proper forms to file to legitimize your LLC. Large states like California will send you back a Forms Packet chock full of instructions and information. For example, California's Secretary of State will provide such documents as—

- Articles of Organization (for newly organized LLCs)
- Articles of Organization-Conversion (from a Non-LLC)
- Amendment of Articles of Organization
- Restated Articles of Organization
- Statement of Information (re managers and owners)
- Designation of Agent for Service of Process
- Service of Process on LLC

... and so on

In addition, in any manner that you can, get access to a complete copy of your state's LLC law. Search the Internet for legal sites and law book publishers. You want a printed and bound text in your hand that you can browse through and read and reference from time to time. Expect to pay $50 to $100 for such a text. You have no intention of becoming an LLC legal expert; you just want to become familiar first-hand with what the law is all about. Obviously, familiarity does not mean reading and memorizing every word of the LLC law. You certainly need to get the general sense of the legal underpinnings of your LLC.

What kind of business can your LLC engage in? Answer: California Section 17002: *Business activity; limitations*, states—

*Subject to any limitations contained in the articles of organization and to compliance with other applicable laws, a limited liability company may engage in **any lawful business activity**, except the banking business, the business of issuing policies of insurance and assuming insurance risks, or the trust company business.* [Emphasis added.]

Except for the exceptions, "any lawful business activity" is quite broad. In fact, it is too broad. For practical reasons, every LLC should narrow its focus to some reasonably achievable business domain. Even though the law may imply so, you can't do everything. And you can't have an unlimited number of manager-owner-members either. Common sense must prevail.

Initiating Documents Required

Section 17050 of California LLC law is titled: *Formation; requirements.* Other states have identical (or nearly so) requirements. The essence of California law reads—

> *In order to form a limited liability company, one or more persons shall execute and file **articles of organization** with, and on a form prescribed by, the Secretary of State and, either before or after the filing of the articles of organization, the members shall have entered into **an operating agreement**. The person or persons who execute and file the articles of organization may, but need not, be members of the limited liability company.* [Emphasis added.]

Note that two separate documents are required: (1) Articles of Organization, and (2) an Operating Agreement. Note that articles of organization are to be on a form prescribed by the Secretary of State. This form, in California, is designated as LLC-1: *Limited Liability Company; Articles of Organization.* The instructions on the back of the form tell you not to alter it; just fill in the blanks. Our abbreviation of an LLC-1 is presented in Figure 9.1. This filled-in form plus a prescribed filing fee are what California initially wants. Other matters follow later.

Meanwhile, it is significant to note that there is no prescribed form for an operating agreement. Why? Because it is up to the LLC members themselves to prepare their own operating agreement form. This is what is meant by "either before or after" the filing of articles of organization . . . *the members **shall have** entered into an operating agreement.* At some point, therefore, all prospective members have to get together at an organization meeting and agree on the elements of their modus operandi.

Within 90 days after the filing of Articles of Organization, California law requires the filing of a statement of information *on a form prescribed by the Secretary of State.* Said prescribed document is **Form LLC-12:** *Limited Liability Company: Statement of Information*. Self-explanatory instructions are on the back. The leadoff instructions tell you that said form is required biennially (every two years) after its initial filing.

State of California **Secretary of State** ◆ **LIMITED LIABILITY COMPANY** *ARTICLES OF ORGANIZATION* Filing Fee $___	File #_____ *Space for State Certification*

1.	Name of company ---------------------------------
2.	Purpose of company (all preprinted; no changes allowed)
3.	Name of agent for service of process: ☐ Individual ☐ Corporation
4.	California address of agent: -------------------------
5.	Company will be managed by: *(Check One)* ☐ one manager ☐ more than one manager ☐ single member LLC ☐ all LLC members
6.	Other matters to be included. Attach separate pages.
7.	Number of pages attached: ------------------------
8.	Type of business: -------------------------------
9.	DECLARATION: by person who executes instrument. *Signature of Organizer* *Type or Print Name* Date: _____
10.	RETURN TO: Name Company Address

California Form LLC - 1

Fig. 9.1 - Condensed Version of California "Prescribed" Form LLC-1

The primary purpose of the Statement of Information is to keep the Secretary of State's LLC files up to date with respect to the—

1. Agent for service of legal process,

2. Principal business activity,

3. Office(s) for maintenance of records, and

4. Names and addresses of **all** members, managers, and CEOs (if any) . . . on attached pages (as necessary).

Persons authorized to execute and sign Form LLC-12 "shall be" any manager (or CEO), attorney in fact, or any member designated by majority vote of the LLC governing body.

We're not sure that you sense the legal significance of what we've just presented to you. Like any business entity, an LLC **is subject** to litigative attack by any customer, supplier, lender, or member who becomes disgruntled or dissatisfied in his/her/its dealings with your LLC. A reasonable cause for lawsuit would exist if there is any failure to comply with ALL of the requirements of applicable state law.

Information to be Maintained

Using California LLC law as an example, we cite its Section 17058. Said section is titled: *Information required to be maintained at office.* The term "at office" means the principal, head, home, or central office of the LLC. If the required information is scattered among various members, managers, and agents, the arrangement would be "out-of-sync" with the statutory requirement for California. We are sure that other states would insist similarly.

California's LLC Section 17058 reads, essentially in full, as follows (with emphasis added):

(a) *Each limited liability company **shall maintain** at the office . . . **all of** the following:*

(1) A current list of the full name and last known business or residence address of each member and of each holder of an economic interest in the LLC set forth in alphabetical order, together with the contribution and the share in profits and losses of each member and holder of an economic interest.

(2) A current list of the full name and business or residence address of each manager.

*(3) A copy of the articles of organization and **all amendments thereto**, together with any powers of attorney pursuant to which the articles of organization or any amendments thereto were executed.*

*(4) Copies of the LLC's **federal**, **state**, **and local income tax or information returns** and reports, if any, for the six **most recent taxable years**.*

*(5) A copy of the LLC's **operating agreement**, if in writing, and any amendments thereto . . .*

*(6) Copies of the **financial statements** of the LLC, if any, for the six most recent fiscal years.*

*(7) The books and records of the LLC as they relate to the **internal affairs** of the company for at least the current and past four fiscal years.*

The tracking, preparing, posting, and maintaining of the above information — **continuously** — is a tall order. It is daunting and burdensome to an LLC whose members are cavalier, procrastinative, and indifferent to recordkeeping chores. This characteristic alone justifies the need for an explicit Operating Agreement . . . IN WRITING. Note that paragraph 17058(a)(5) above refers to such agreement as: *if in writing.* If not in writing, can't you see the finger-pointing among members when responsibility questions arise, finances are low, and assets are disbursed? This is reckless exposure of your jugular vein, when legal adversaries start their drum beat and war dance.

Cash Starvation by Members

There is one critical area where an operating agreement can prove its worth. It is the matter of capital contributions to, shortages of, and withdrawals from company assets. Virtually every small- and medium-sized business tends to be capital starved. An LLC, with members who are fascinated with misconceptions of the limited liability concept, is particularly susceptible to the cash starvation process. A responsibly adopted operating agreement can forestall — and possibly prevent — the premature termination of an enterprise based on capital deficiencies alone. On this premise, California LLC Sections 17200 and 17201 are instructive.

Section 17200: *Capital contributions*, reads in part—

The operating agreement may provide for capital contributions of members. [Such contributions] *may be in money, property, or services, or **other obligation** to contribute money or property or to render services.* [Emphasis added.]

Note in the citation above the term: "obligation to . . .". Said obligation is spelled out in Section 17201: ***Obligation to contribute cash, property, or services*** (etc.). This section reads in its most significant part as—

*Subject to the terms of the operating agreement, a member is **not excused** from an obligation . . . to perform any promise to contribute cash or property or to perform services because of death, disability, dissolution, or any other reason. . . . An operating agreement may provide that the* [ownership] *interest of a member who fails to make any contributions or other payment that the member is required to make **will be subject** to specific remedies for, or specific consequences of, the failure. . . . The specific remedies or consequences may include loss of voting, approval, or other rights; loss of the member's ability to participate in the management and operations of the company or its liquidated damages; or **a reduction of** the defaulting member's **economic rights**.* [Emphasis added.]

In other words, an LLC has the power to financially discipline its own members. Failure to do so, when economic prudence requires, could be construed as prima facie evidence that the LLC is functioning as a sham.

Can't you sense the flood of legal actions against your LLC should it exercise its business powers without obligating all members to come forth financially? Of all the opportunistic features of an LLC, we think that failure to obligate members to maintain an adequate capital base is an LLC's most vulnerable weakness. The "LL" is not a license for cavalierness.

The "Alter Ego Liability" Rule

The doctrine of alter ego liability is one of long standing. It has evolved from the many abuses of closely-held entities, such as corporations, partnerships, and trusts. And, now, closely-held LLCs. The term "closely held" means five or fewer individuals owning 50% or more of the controlling interests of an entity. In these situations, the distinction between entity business and personal business is blurred and commingled. To invoke the alter ego doctrine, it has to be shown that the entity was a mere conduit for the transaction of personal business and that no separate identity of the individual and the entity really existed.

The lack of separate identity stands out starkly when there is commingling of funds, disguise of expenditures, unrestrained drawdown of capital, poor recordkeeping, lavish travel and entertainment, and the like. Owner self-discipline in separating business from personal matters is minimal or nonexistent. The entity formulation and use of its registered name is an "ego thing" for the close owners. Often, state registration as an LLC is used to taunt and distract an otherwise bona fide litigant.

Following through with citing portions of California LLC law as an example, we cite its Section 17101(b): *Liability of members; alter ego*. This section expressly states that—

*A member of an LLC **shall be subject** to liability under the common law governing alter ego liability, **and shall also** be personally liable under a judgment of a court **or for** any debt, obligation, or liability of the LLC, whether that liability or obligation arises in contract, tort, or otherwise, **under the same or similar circumstances** and to the same extent **as a shareholder of a corporation** may be personally liable.* [Emphasis added.]

There is no wiggle room here. Once it can be shown that there is no distinct line of separation between the entity and one or more of its members, each such member becomes subject to personal liability. It is the de facto act or acts that count legally. For example, the operating agreement prohibits any personal transactions on company letterhead, writing company checks, or using company equipment. Nevertheless, some senior member goes ahead and makes his monthly mortgage payments on his personal home with company checks. Doing so, he has snagged the trip wire into alter ego liability. There are other elements of LLC mismanagement that can cause trip-wire snagging. So important is this doctrine that we depict it in Figure 9.2.

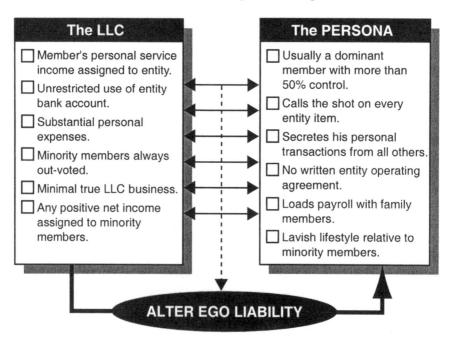

Fig. 9.2 - Elements of Indistinguishability Between Entity and Persona

It is important to be aware that, if one member acquires alter ego liability, he carries his burden alone. Other members are unaffected unless they, too, ignore the separability doctrine of entity vs. persona. It is easy to ignore this doctrine in the expectation euphoria of LLC status.

Single-Member Tax Filings

As indicated previously, many states — but not all — authorize single-member LLCs. In California, the specific citation on point [Sec. 17050(b)] reads—

A limited liability company shall have one or more members.

Of particular note at this point is that the IRS does **not** recognize a single-member LLC. For IRS tax filing purposes, such an LLC is a **disregarded entity**. That is, the "entity" aspect is disregarded, and the single member owner files a *proprietorship* return: Schedule C (Form 1040) [Recall Chapter 7].

To indicate to the IRS that your proprietorship is a state-authorized LLC, you add the letters "LLC" to your fictitious business name entered on Schedule C (1040).

As a proprietorship LLC, the state in which you are franchised to do business requires its own tax form. In the case of California (CA), for example, the applicable tax filing is: **CA Form 568**: *Limited Liability Company Return of Income*. It is a 4-page form accompanied by 48 pages of instructions. It is more than just an information return; it is a return of **tax**. It accommodates four types of such taxes, namely:

[1] An LLC annual minimum tax
[2] An LLC *fee* based on total income
[3] A nonresident member's tax, and
[4] A *Use Tax* for out-of-state purchases

On page 1 of CA Form 568, you are directed to—

Enter the maximum number of members in the LLC at any time during the year ▶ _____. *Attach a California Schedule K-1 (568) for each of these members.*

This entry is followed by 13 Yes-No checkbox questions. All such questions are designed to hold your feet to the fire with respect to fulfilling all LLC requirements under state law. Any failure to do so defaults you into a "disregarded entity" status.

Also accompanying CA Form 568 is a Schedule L: **Balance Sheets**. Though technically not required by a single-member LLC whose total receipts are less than $250,000 we urge, nevertheless, the completion of Schedule L. Nothing is more surprising to alter ego antagonists than an LLC having an iron-clad set of books of account (income and expenses), a complete tabulation of assets and liabilities, and individual capital accounts all balanced out.

Multi-Member Tax Filings

When two or more unincorporated LLC members associate in a profit-seeking venture, they are automatically construed to be a general partnership. This is the treatment accorded to both federal and state tax filings. A general partnership has no limited liability protections. For federal filings, IRS form 1065 is required. We introduced you to Form 1065 in Chapter 8.

The additional information we need to add is your response to Question 1 on Schedule B (1065): *Other Information.* The Question 1 asks—

What type of entity is filing this return?

☐ *Domestic limited liability company (LLC)*
☐ *Domestic limited liability partnership (LLP)*
☐ ... or 1 of 4 other checkboxes

If you check either the LLC or LLP box, you must also prepare and file IRS Form 8832: **Entity Classification Election**. Check the "Form of entity" box there that reads—

☐ *A domestic eligible entity electing to be classed as a partnership*

This tells the IRS that you have registered with your home state as an LL (limited liability) entity. We introduced you to Form 8832 in the latter part of Chapter 6.

In California, as in many other states, there are registration and tax distinctions between an LLC and an LLP. The C-type LL is an ordinary trade or business doing business within (and perhaps outside of) the registering state. An LLC cannot engage in the professions of law, accounting, architecture, medicine, and other professions requiring advanced degrees and special (state) licenses. These professions are the domain of LLPs: the "P" is for professional partnerships.

Whether an LLC or LLP, each entity files federal Form 1065: *U.S. Return of Partnership Income*. In California, an LLC files **CA Form 568** introduced earlier. An LLP files **CA Form 565** which is almost a mirror image of Form 1065.

In either case, LLC or LLP, the *economic substance* rule must prevail; that is, no member-partner can excuse himself from his pro rata share of the operating liabilities of the LL entity. The term "operating liabilities" refers to those normal contractual obligations to customers, clients, vendors, suppliers, and employees. To assure meeting these obligations, each member's capital participation must be monitored continuously. A depiction of our point in this regard is presented in Figure 9.3.

LLC Pros and Cons

Though some states recognize single-member LLCs, all states recognize multi-member LLCs. Multi-member LLCs have all of the operating flexibility and tax benefit pass-throughs of a general partnership. But they have one additional advantage. The personal liability of each participant is limited by the LLC law of the registering state. The objective of each LLC law is to separate the personal liability of each member from the entity liability of all members. All LLC laws are premised on multi-membership in an unincorporated entity referred to, simply, as an LLC.

Unfortunately, an LLC tends to attract shrewd and cunning members. Such persons are the types who want everything in their favor. They seek to time their entry into and withdrawal from the LLC just before *and* just after a major entity transaction takes place. For example, the LLC sells its small shopping center for $1,000,000. After taking into account the entity's adjusted basis in the property and its selling expenses, the entity's capital gain is $600,000, say. Just 10 days before the sale, a shrewd member plunks down $100,000 as additional contribution to his existing capital. As of the date of sale, he has a 50% ownership interest in the LLC. Just 10 days after the sale, he withdraws his $100,000 and demands $300,000 of the capital gain as his "distributive share" of the proceeds. Come on, now: $300,000 for a 20-day voluntary loan to the LLC. How unreasonable can one be? To con artists, reasonableness is not a feature of their temperament.

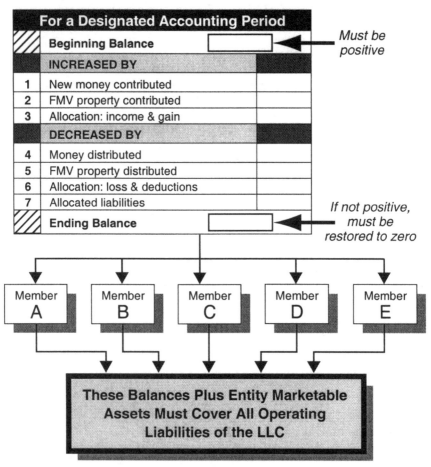

Fig. 9.3 - Mechanics of Partners' Capital Accounting for a Solvent LLC

Consequently, if the demands are not met immediately, the egregious member threatens to get an attorney and tear apart the LLC operating agreement. He already knows that the agreement has no prohibition whatsoever against his 20-day incursion strategy. He knows this because it was *he* who diverted attention from any such provision in the agreement.

LIMITED LIABILITY COMPANY			
	ADVANTAGES		DISADVANTAGES
1.	Universal appeal of "Limited Liability" when conducting business in unincorporated form within home state.	1.	Requires state registration on prescribed forms; payment of annual fees; updates on members for "legal process."
2.	Can conduct any business not otherwise illegal or restricted by business activity laws of registering state.	2.	Must maintain regular books of account re income, expenses, assets, & liabilities; federal & state tax treatment often differ.
3.	No limit to number of LLC members, provided each signs (in good faith) the "Operating Agreement".	3.	Tends to attract con artists and cavalier participants who prey on loopholes in the agreement.
4.	No tax to LLC entity at time of formation, nor at time of distribution, if all events verified and documented.	4.	Each member's tax basis & ownership interest must be monitored with "mandatory adjustments", in & out.
5.	Registry in home state permits doing business in other LLC states, under reciprocity principles.	5.	Requires registration in non-resident states & compliance with their tax & liability laws.
6.	Ease of mergers with & conversions into other more formal forms of business, such as C corps & spin-offs.	6.	Organizational changes "too easy"; leads to sloppy record-keeping & oversights in registry protections; invites vindictive lawsuits.

Fig. 9.4 - Other Pros and Cons of an LLC

There is really only one way to handle the above matter and others like it. Limit a member's participation in entity transactional gains or losses to the percentage of days a member participated during the total holding-period days that the property was owned by the entity.

Let us illustrate. Suppose that in the 20-day incursion example above, the shopping center was held by the LLC for 1,000 days before it was sold. The percentage of incursion participation in the property holding would be 10 days divided by 1,000 days, or 1%. The con artist gets no transaction credit for remaining in the LLC for 10 days after the property was sold. Thus, instead of the $300,000 ($600,000 x 50%) he demanded by threatening a lawsuit, he would be entitled to just 1% of the $600,000 gain or $6,000 only. Does **your** LLC operating agreement cover situations like this? If not, why not? This example happens all the time when there's a legal sharpie in the herd.

The long and short herein is that a multi-member LLC has to prepare all of the federal tax forms and Schedules K-1 of a partnership. There is no LLC federal form as there is with LLC state forms. To refresh your recollection of federal partnership features, a skim review of Chapter 8 would be helpful.

In the meantime, for summary and checklist purposes, other advantages and disadvantages of an LLC are presented in Figure 9.4. In short, an LLC is not a front or disguise for avoiding all legal liability in the ordinary cause of a for-profit trade or business.

10

S CORPORATION: FORM 1120S

Becoming An S Corporation Is A TAX ELECTION Process: Not An Incorporation Process. Under State Law, The Entity Is A General Corporation And Must Conduct Its Affairs As Such. The S Status Election Requires IRS Form 2553 Whereon All Shareholders Must Consent UNANIMOUSLY. Thereafter, Form 1120S Is Filed With As Many Schedules K-1 Attached As There Are Individual Shareholders. All Core Business Income And Deductions Appear On Page 1, Whereas Its Financial Status (Assets And Liabilities) Appears On Page 4. Pages 2 And 3 Consist Of "Distributive Share" Items That Pass Through To Shareholders.

When a small business entity incorporates under the General Corporation Law of any state, the IRS regards that entity, per se, as a C corporation. While most states recognize S corporations, there are no special provisions in state law to incorporate as such. There is a practical reason for this. The distinction between a C corporation and an S corporation is the TAX TREATMENT: **not** the incorporation treatment. Consequently, becoming an S corporation is a tax election by the shareholders of the incorporated entity. Those states that recognize S corporations for tax purposes follow the federal requirements for becoming an S.

A corporation that has no more than 100 shareholders *may elect* to become an S corporation. Upon such an election, the corporation itself is not subject to income tax, as in the case of a C corporation. Instead, the S corporation income is passed through and directly taxed to its shareholders. As a result, an S corporation becomes a *pass-through* entity much like that of a partnership.

The elective choice to be an S corporation is statutorily allowed in order to minimize the effect of taxation on deciding whether to be a corporation or a partnership. A corporation has limited liability. Thus, when electing to be an S corporation, shareholders get the tax benefits of a partnership along with the limited liability benefits of a corporation. This very special treatment applies only to small business corporations where the term "small" means 100 or fewer shareholders.

Accordingly, in this chapter we want to focus on the characteristics of an S corporation, how the election to become so is made, who are "eligible shareholders," and what federal tax forms are required during and after the first operating year.

Subchapter S Overview

In case you may have wondered about it, where does the assignment of an "S" status come from? As stated above, the distinction is not made under state law; it is made under federal tax law — the Internal Revenue Code — only.

The "S" comes from *Subchapter S* of the IR Code. Said subchapter is fully titled: ***Tax Treatment of S Corporations and Their Shareholders***. Subchapter S spans Sections 1361 through 1379, some 14 tax code sections in all. These 14 sections, consisting of approximately 14,000 statutory words, are subtitled as presented in Figure 10.1. A quick glance should convince you that all we can do here is to touch on only the highlights of Subchapter S.

Editorial Note: If you recall from the previous chapter re LLCs, we did not identify any specific sections of the tax code that address LLCs. This is because there are none. An LLC is primarily a state law matter. Its federal recognition arises from IRS Regulation § 301.7701-3: *Classification of certain business entities* and from Form 8832: *Entity Classification Election.*

An S corporation is defined almost exclusively by its number and type of shareholders, rather than by its amount of capitalization, gross receipts, or business activities. The basic requisite is that it be an *active domestic* corporation organized for profit purposes. It is not a passive investment vehicle.

U.S. Code	Title 26 - INTERNAL REVENUE CODE	
	Subtitle A - INCOME TAXES	
	Chapter 1 - Normal Taxes & Surtaxes	
	Subchapter S - Tax Treatment of S Corporation	
Section	Section Titles	Subsections
	Part I - In General	
1361	S Corporation Defined	(a) . . . (e)
1362	Election; Revocation; Termination	(a) . . . (g)
1363	Effect of Election on Corporation	(a) . . . (d)
	Part II - Tax Treatment of Shareholders	
1366	Pass-Thru of Items	(a) . . . (f)
1367	Adjustments to Stock Basis	(a) . . . (b)
1368	Distributions	(a) . . . (e)
	Part III - Special Rules	
1371	Coordination with Subchapter C	(a) . . . (e)
1372	Partnership Fringe Benefit Rules	(a) . . . (b)
1373	Foreign Income	(a) . . . (b)
1374	Tax on Built-in Gains	(a) . . . (e)
1375	Tax on Passive Investment Income	(a) . . . (d)
	Part IV - Miscellaneous	
1377	Definitions & Special Rule	(a) . . . (c)
1378	Taxable Year of S Corporation	(a) . . . (b)
1379	Transitional Rules on Enactment	(a) . . . (e)

Fig. 10.1 - Tax Code Sections Relating to S Corporation Status

The parameters of an S corporation are prescribed in Section 1361: *S Corporation Defined*. Subsection 1361(a)(1) says—

*The term "S corporation" means, **with respect to any taxable year**, a small business corporation for which **an election** under section 1362(a) **is in effect** for such year.* [Emphasis added.]

As the emphasized terms imply, S status is a tax year to tax year affair. And, then, only after a shareholder election has been held. But let the election wane or become disqualified in some way, the entity reverts to a C corporation . . . automatically.

Subsection 1361(b)(1) supports the above by saying that a "small business corporation" means—

*a domestic corporation which is not an ineligible corporation and **which does not have**—*

(A) more than 100 shareholders,
(B) as a shareholder a person . . . who is not an individual,
(C) a nonresident alien as a shareholder, and
(D) more than 1 class of stock. [Be sure to read this clause as "not" more than.]

Partnerships, LLCs, and C corporations cannot be shareholders. These are entities and, thus, are not individuals. However, domestic family trusts — when individually created and controlled — can become shareholders in an S corporation.

Counting the Shareholders

For most small and closely-held corporations, the number of shareholders is not particularly significant. It rarely comes up to 100. But in highly touted and widely held small businesses expecting to grow big, the number 100 can be reached quite easily. This is especially true where there are a number of husband and wife owners, a number of trusts with multiple beneficiaries, and a new phenomenon called: Qualified Subchapter S Trusts (QSSTs). In these situations, how do you count the number of shareholders?

First off, subsection 1361(c)(1) says that—

a husband and wife (and their estates) shall be treated as 1 shareholder.

An "estate" comprises the assets of a deceased individual. It exists for a limited period of time (6 to 15 months) while the estate is being inventoried, appraised, and settled. At time of settlement, the assets (after debts and expenses are paid) are distributed either directly to individual heirs, or into a trust for piecemeal distributions to them over a number of years.

So long as a husband and wife are married (whether they live together or not) at the time S status is voted upon, they count as one shareholder. If they become divorced, and each owns shares in the corporation, they are two shareholders. If the count was exactly 100 at the time of the election (when they were married), and they became divorced after the election, that would be 101 shareholders. Inadvertently, the S election becomes disqualified. This is a technicality that has to be astutely addressed by management. If, instead of a divorce, one of the spouses dies, the one shareholder count holds.

In the case of shares held in trust, the trust itself generally counts as one shareholder. This is especially true if there is only one current beneficiary of the trust. The trustee is the person who makes the election for or against S status.

If there are two or more current beneficiaries of a trust, and each is a substantial beneficial owner of the assets thereof (income and capital), a counting problem arises. Suppose, for example, that there are three current beneficiaries (A, B, and C) owning equally one-third of the trust. Is the trust treated as one shareholder, or is it treated as three shareholders?

Answer: It depends. If the books of account were set up as subtrust A, subtrust B, and subtrust C, and separate trust tax returns were filed for the year of the election, a case could be made that there were three shareholders: not one. There would be a problem, though, if one of the three beneficiaries disapproved of the S status election. As you'll see below, he alone would have veto power over 99 other shareholders who might approve of the S election. Allowing any one person veto power can cause endless acrimony and lawsuits.

Unanimous Consent Required

Section 1362 is titled: *Election; Revocation; Termination* (of S status]. Approximately 2,800 tax law words are used. At the moment, our concern is the election process under subsection (a). This subsection reads in full, as follows:

   (1)   *Except as provided in subsection (g)* [re the 5-year wait period after termination], *a small business corporation*

> *may elect, in accordance with the provision of this section, to be an S corporation.*
>
> *(2)   An election under this subsection shall be valid **only if all** persons who are **shareholders** in such corporation on the day on which the election is made **consent to such election**.* [Emphasis added.]

In other words, unanimous consent must be attained on the date of the election. This can be a Herculean task when there are 15, 35, 50 or more shareholders involved. Controversies can erupt because of differences in tax interests. A high income shareholder may not want any S corporation profits passed through to him, though he probably would want the losses to pass through. Conversely, a low income shareholder would certainly want the profits passed through, but not the losses.

To minimize shareholder controversy concerning their own individual taxes, it is best to seek S status when there are 15 or fewer shareholders involved. Section 1362(a) requires unanimous consent only "on the day which" the election is made. Once an S election is valid, new shareholders are not required to consent to the election. Nor can they terminate an election by objecting to it, or by refusing to accept its pass-through tax treatment.

At the time of the election, each eligible shareholder must read and sign (and date) the following IRS-prepared consent statement:

> *Under penalties of perjury, we declare that we consent to the election of the above-named corporation to be an S corporation under section 1362(a) and that we have examined this consent statement, including accompanying schedules and statements, and to the best of our knowledge and belief, it is true, correct, and complete.* ***We understand that our consent is binding and may not be withdrawn after the corporation has made a valid election.*** [Emphasis added.]

/s/_____	(date)
/s/_____	(date)
/s/_____	(date)
etc.	etc.

Elect on Form 2553

As you would expect, there is a special IRS form for making the S status election. It is Form 2553: **_Election by a Small Business Corporation_**. Although arranged in three parts, it is Part I: **_Election Information_**, that is most pertinent here. The form is accompanied by approximately 3,600 words of instructions. Completing the form is serious tax legal business. Because so, each shareholder should be given a blank copy of Form 2553 (front and back) before seeking his/her signature on it.

As partly edited, preprinted headnotes on Form 2553 read:

1. *This election to be an S corporation can be accepted **only if all** [8] tests are met under **Who May Elect** on page 1 of the instructions. All signatures [must be] originals (no photocopies).*

2. *Do not file [a tax return] for an S corporation for any year before the election takes effect.*

3. *If the corporation was in existence before the effective date of this election, see **Taxes an S Corporation May Owe** [in] the instructions.*

The required Election Information in Part I is entered onto 14 alphabetized lines and columns. For instructional overview, we list the captions of these 14 entry items.

A. Employer identification number
B. Date incorporated
C. State of incorporation
D. Effective tax year of election
E. Name of person for IRS contact
F. Phone number for IRS contact
G. If corporation name or address change, ☐
H. Earliest of 3 dates if election is for first year of operation
I. Selected taxable year (If other than a calendar year, complete Part II)
J. Name/address each shareholder

K. Shareholders' consent statements
L. Number of shares; date acquired
M. Shareholders' Tax IDs
N. End of each shareholder's tax year

For shareholder familiarization purposes, the general format of Form 2553 is presented in Figure 10.2.

Form 2553	ELECTION BY SMALL BUSINESS CORPORATION - Under Sec. 1362 of IR Code			
3 Headnotes: See Text				
Part I	ELECTION INFORMATION			

	Corporation Name, Address, City, State, ZIP	A	EIN
		B	Date incorporated
		C	State of incorporation

D	Tax year for which election effective		mo / day / yr
E	Name, address, of person to contact	F	Phone Number
G	Change of name or address after applying for EIN		▶□
H	If effective 1st year of operation, enter **earliest date of**: (1) 1st shareholders, (2) 1st assets, or (3) 1st business mo / day / yr		
I	Select tax year: Ending month _____ - if other than calendar year, complete Part II		

J	K		L		M	N
Name, address each shareholder	**CONSENT STATEMENT**		Shares held		SSN each s/h	Each s/h tax year ends
	signature	date	number	date		
	Use Continuation Sheets as Needed					

Authenticating Officer _____ *signature / title / date*

Part II	Selection of Fiscal Tax Year
Part III	Qualified Subchapter S Trust Election

Fig. 10.2 - General Contents of Form 2553: Election of S Status

Although the instructions do not require so, we think it a good idea for every signing shareholder to receive a photocopy of the election form, once it is certified by a responsible officer of the corporation. A requirement to do so could be specified in the bylaws, thereby hopefully avoiding subsequent controversy.

Upon attaining unanimous consents, and authentication by a responsible officer — the President or Secretary, usually — the election form is sent to the IRS Service Center designated in the instructions. It is sent solo **without** other tax forms attached.

Must First Incorporate

In case you've missed the point, before executing IRS Form 2553, you and your associates must be incorporated. The process is rather routine. You contact the Secretary of State, Corporations Division, in the state where you intend to do business (at least initially). You'll probably have to go on the Internet, as rarely does a human being ever answer a business phone these days. You'll be sent an *Articles of Incorporation* forms package with preparatory instructions. With the samples provided, you can prepare your own articles and submit them. Or, you can engage a professional incorporator (attorney or accountant) to do the initial paperwork for you.

There will be a filing fee . . . order of a few $100. After the Articles and fee are received, a state corporation number will be assigned. Subsequent thereto, a *Certificate of Incorporation* with the state seal thereon will be issued. You'll also be assigned a corporation number that, at the state level, is comparable to an EIN (Employer/Entity ID) at the federal level. In Figure 10.3 we present a pictograph of the process involved.

With your incorporation certificate at hand, you and your associates have to adopt a set of Bylaws (for managing the business), designate your initial Board of Directors, elect a Secretary, call a meeting of initial shareholders, keep Minutes thereon, and prepare a Shareholders Ledger. At some point in this stage, you'll have to determine the amount of initial capitalization required and the total number of shares (and share certificates) to be authorized. Make sure that your initial capitalization will at least cover the first three years of operation.

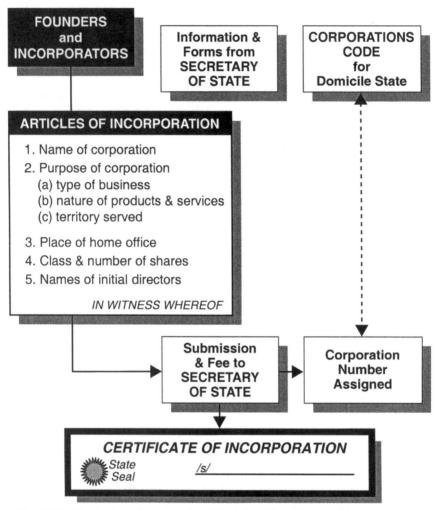

Fig. 10.3 - Basic Requirements for Obtaining "Certificate of Incorporation"

Use caution when issuing share certificates. First off, they will be *private* shares. They cannot be offered to nor sold to the general public. Even so, you'll probably need to file an *Information Notice* with the Corporate Securities Regulation division of your state of incorporation. Find out, as an S corporation, how many shares and total capitalization you can authorize, and be exempt from the public registration requirements.

Typically, the exempt figure is less than 300,000 shares or so, and capitalization less than $3,000,000 (3 million) or so. In California, for example, the exempt threshold is 35 or fewer shareholders, each with less than $1,000,000 in total assets. Better check on this matter carefully. Nothing is more devastating to the startup synergy of a new corporation than being hammered by corporate securities law violations.

Overview of Form 1120S

Once incorporation and shares matters are out of the way, you can give attention to IRS Form 1120S. Its full title is: *U.S. Income Tax Return for an S Corporation*. It consists basically of four pages plus a Schedule K-1 for each consenting shareholder. A Schedule K-1 (Form 1120S) is the pass-through of each shareholder's pro rata share of income, deductions, and credits. The 1120S is accompanied by approximately 50 pages of instructions totaling some 64,000 words. If the entity is a newly formed S corporation, the 1120S format closely resembles that of a partnership return of income: Form1065. Recall Chapter 8 on this point. When newly formed, there is no S corporation tax.

If newly incorporated, and IRS election Form 2553 is executed within 2 1/2 months of incorporation, the initial year of business operation coincides with the accounting year of choice of the shareholders [IRC Sec. 1362(b)(1)(B)]. In this case, in the head portion of Form 1120S, you check the applicable box at line F(1) ☐ *Initial return.*

If the shareholders delay more than 2 1/2 months in executing Form 2553, you must operate as a C corporation. During your initial year or whatever subsequent year you can obtain unanimous consent, you can convert to an S corporation. When converting from a C to an S, three "conversion taxes" may apply, namely:

a. Excess net passive income tax
   — when more than 25% of gross income is from passive investment sources;

b. Tax on built-in capital gains
   — when appreciated C corporation assets are sold, and

c. Recapture tax on investment credits and change in inventory accounting methods.

Otherwise, page 1 of Form 1120S limits an S corporation's income to its core business, via such entries as:

1. Gross receipts or sales   _____

2. Less returns and allowances   <   >

3. Less cost of goods sold   <   >

4. Plus net ordinary gain/<loss> from
   Form 4797: *Sales of Business Property*   _____

5. Plus other income/<loss>, attach schedule   _____

Adding lines 1 through 5 establishes an S corporation's **Total income**. Thereafter, the deductions portion of page 1 of Form 1120S includes those ordinary and necessary expenses which are allowable to all forms of active trade or business.

Page 2 of Form 1120S consists of Schedule A: *Cost of Goods Sold* and Schedule B: *Other Information.* We covered Schedule A matters back in Chapter 3. The "Other Information" covers method of accounting, product or service, whether a tax shelter, whether converted from a C corporation, accumulated earnings and profits (if any), and whether total receipts and assets for the year are less than $250,000. If more than $250,000, the Schedules L and M balance sheets on page 4 must be completed. This is the same balance-sheet-completing threshold for general partnerships. For limited liability protection, it is our position that corporate balance sheets should be completed regardless of the entity's magnitude of receipts and assets. Balance sheeting requires good accounting discipline that helps to validate the corporate shield.

For best comprehension of the scope of Form 1120S we urge that you procure an official copy of it with instructions. Since approximately 50 pages are involved, it is better to order by phone rather than downloading it from the IRS's website. When phoning (1-800-829-3676) ask for **Package 1120S**.

Schedule D (Form 1120S)

In the S corporation's "Forms package," you will note a Schedule D: *Capital Gains and Losses and Built-in Gains*. The Schedule D consists of Part I: Short-Term (one year or less), Part II: Long-Term (more than one year) and Part III: Built-in Gains (when converting from a C to an S corporation). If there is no C to S conversion, Part III does not apply.

If, in Parts I and/or II there is a net gain or <loss>, it is **not** transferred to the income portion of Form 1120S. Instead, it is transferred to Schedule K of Form 1120S. Schedule K is titled: *Shareholders' Share of Income, Deductions, Credits, etc.* From Schedule K, a Schedule K-1 is prepared for each individual shareholder. Why so?

Answer: Because an S corporation is a pass-through entity. That is, all tax attributes — except built-in gains from C corporation conversions — pass through directly to the shareholders. Only when there is a C corporation conversion does an S corporation pay any tax.

Schedule K, incidentally, takes up the lower 1/3 of page 2 of Form 1120S, and all of its page 3. There are 57 lines of entry information on Schedule K. These 57 lines are sectioned into—

- Income <Loss>   [15 lines]
- Deductions   [6 lines]
- Credits & Recaptures   [7 lines]
- Foreign Transactions   [13 lines]
- Alternative Tax Items   [6 lines]
- Shareholder Basis Items   [5 lines]
- Other Information   [5 lines]

The 15 lines of income <loss> information on Schedule K infer that, in addition to its active core business, an S corporation can engage in any passive or any investment activity that the Board of Directors approves.

From Schedule K to Schedule K-1

Schedule K (1120S) addresses the distributive sharing (pass-through) items for all shareholders collectively. Each Schedule K entry is then apportioned to each shareholder individually as per his/her *percentage of stock ownership* for the year. For example, suppose an item on Schedule K was $7,000. Also, suppose that one particular shareholder's percentage ownership was 3.572% (0.03572). If so, the entry amount on Schedule K-1 would be $250 [$7,000 x 0.03572]. And so on down each entry amount on Schedule K that is transferred to Schedule K-1.

Schedule K-1 (1120S): each *Shareholder's Share*, etc. exactly mirrors all entry items on Schedule K. The format is different, but the line numbers exact match. In Figure 10.4 we show the general arrangement of a K-1. What we don't show — and can't show — is the back side of Schedule K-1: its page 2. The page 2 lists approximately 100 "Enter on Form 1040" directions.

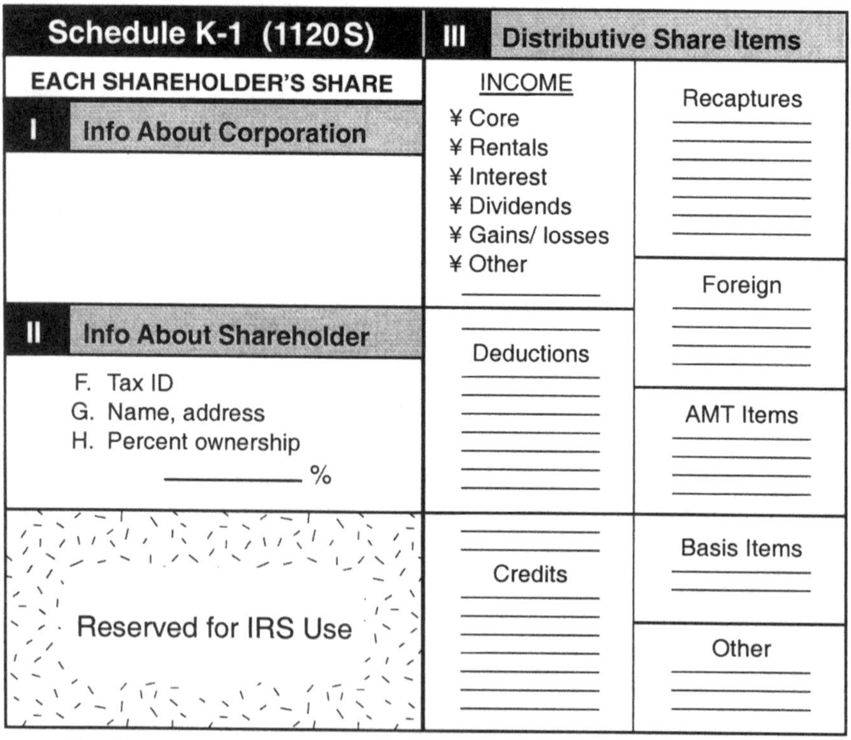

Fig. 10.4 - Arrangement of Schedule K-1 Attached to Form 1120S)

A bold-printed headnote at the top of page 2 reads—

This list identifies the codes used for all shareholders and provides summarized information for shareholders who file Form 1040 [or Form 1041 for trusts].

Another important instruction on page 2 reads—

Ordinary business income <loss>. You must first determine whether the income <loss> is passive or nonpassive.

If you have net passive losses (e.g., from rental real estate activities), your loss writeoffs from all passive activities are limited to <$25,000> per taxpayer-shareholder.

As indicated in Figure 10.4, there's a Part II: *Information about the Shareholder* (singular). There are spaces for entering a participant's ID (SSN or EIN if a trust), his/her full name and address, and his/her percentage of stock ownership: item H. Officially, item H reads in full as—

H. *Shareholder's percentage of stock ownership for tax year*
_____%

Here, the term "for tax year" means for the **full** tax year. But suppose one late S corporation consenter were a shareholder for only 275 days (9 months) of the year. Using the example percentage of 3.572% above, what would the late comer's full year percentage be?

Answer: $3.572\% \times \dfrac{275 \text{ days}}{365 \text{ d/yr}}$

$= 3.572\% \times 0.7531 = 2.689\%$ (or 0.02689)

Item H requires that complete details on each shareholder's participation be maintained at all times. Information such as: $ in, $ out; date in, date out; shares issued, shares redeemed; . . and so on. Always be leery of the shareholder who comes on board late in the year (when the income and pass-through benefits are "on target") and plunks down a wad of money. He expects — demands — a K-1 with disproportionate benefits for less than a full year's participation.

A summary of the above and other advantages and disadvantages of an S-corporation are presented in Figure 10.5.

S CORPORATION	
ADVANTAGES	**DISADVANTAGES**
1. A legal corporate entity under home state law; the "S" implies "small business" where as few as 1,2, or 3 owners may be involved.	1. Requires formal application to Secretary of State, filing of Articles of Incorporation, & payment of registration fee; Certificate of Incorporation issued.
2. The "S" is a Tax Election process where fewer than 100 shareholders agree unanimously; easier with 15 than with 100.	2. Although authorized stock is "private", still must file Information Notice with incorporating state; must avoid public offerings & public sale of stock..
3. Domestic entity with only one class of stock; individuals only (no entities except certain trusts); fosters simplicity & flexibility in business operation.	3. Requires a closely-monitored Shareholder's Ledger with accurate dates, # of shares issued, capital contributions, share redemptions, & shareholder days per each year.
4. More manpower & money available for running the core business; may also engage in passive activities (real estate rentals) & public investment activities.	4. If too many "side" activities, the core business falters, raising tax questions whether more stringent tax shelter & personal holding company rules apply.
5. Has all the pass-through benefits of a partnership or LLC, yet in full corporate form; attractive for new business ventures.	5. The pass-through accounting discipline required can get sloppy, leading to K-1 innacuracies, contentious "capital calls" for undercapitalization offsets.
6. Except when converting from C corp status, the S entity itself pays no federal income tax; thus, all earnings & profits can be "passed through".	6. Up to 3 types of federal conversion taxes may apply; many states also assert a "minimum tax" for the corporate franchise privilege within their state.

Fig. 10.5 - Other Pros and Cons of an S Corporation

11

C CORPORATION: FORM 1120

A C Corporation Is A Separate Taxable Entity Of Its Own. The Amount Of Tax Is Computed On Form 1120, Filed Each Fiscal Year. This Form Consists Of 4 Pages, 12 Subschedules, And Numerous Other Attachments (Such As Loss Carrybacks And Carryforwards). Owner-Officers Must Pay Themselves A Salary And Report Same (Plus Their Fringe Benefits) On Form W-2. For Taxable Incomes Over $100,000, Corporate Tax Rates "Jump All Over The Place" . . . From 15% To 35% . . . Plus Certain "Surtaxes." Personal Service And Personal Holding Corporations Are Subject To A Flat (Nongraduated) Rate Of 35%.

Unlike a partnership, an LLC, or an S corporation, a C corporation is a taxable entity in and of itself. As such, there is a separate legal barrier between the assets and liabilities of the corporation and those of its officers, employees, and stockholders. If a C corporation performs its accounting and reporting functions conscientiously — with no self-dealing games — the limited liability of its stockholders is automatic. In the worst case liability scenario, barring fraud and other malicious acts, the stockholders lose only their capital investment. Their personal homes, bank accounts, and other stock holdings are reasonably protected.

Because of the C corporate shield protection, a new business can attract more officers (and their capital) and more other peoples' money (as ordinary stockholders). With more owner-contributed money, a C business can engage in a wider variety of activities and risks than other forms that are shoestring capitalized. For purposes of this book, we limit our discussion strictly to small C corporations. By "small" we mean an entity whose total assets are less than $10,000,000 (10 million).

For IRS purposes, the C corporation document of focus is **Form 1120**. It is fully titled: *U.S. Corporation Income Tax Return*. There is one particular feature to note in this title. The designation as a "C" corporation does not appear. This is because it is a *general* corporation when incorporated under state law. The incorporation process is identical to that which we covered in the preceding chapter and pictorialized as Figure 10.3 (on page 10-10).

In one sense, there is some tax simplicity in the C Form 1120. Everything is handled by the corporation. It has its own separate books of account (no pass-throughs involved); it has its own separate tax year (which is on a fiscal basis of its choosing); and it is a "taxpayer" strictly independent of its owners and their taxpaying interests. If managed properly, a C corporation can facilitate business growth more flexibly than any other form of new-start entity. Unless intended otherwise, it has indefinite life.

Caution When "Closely-Held"

There is no upper or lower tax limit to the number of stockholders in a C corporation. There can be as few as one to well over 1,000. There are, however, regulatory restrictions re federal and state corporate securities laws when the stock is offered to the general public. When offered only to family members and close friends, the corporation becomes characterized as "closely-held." The entity then becomes tax suspect.

Many small C corporations are created in the belief that their owners can perform tax magic behind the corporate shield. They use the corporation as a game of self-dealing in which many personal, nonbusiness expenses are written off against the corporate income. If the corporation makes money, they buy luxury cars and recreational facilities in the corporate name, but only the owners and their family members can use them. If the corporation builds up accumulated earnings, the owners start borrowing from the corporation. They borrow at below-market interest rates or at no interest at all. The loans are seldom paid back to the corporation; they are rolled over year after year. All the while, the owners pay no income tax on the perpetual borrowings from their own corporation. When doing so, two tax questions emerge: **One**. Is the corporation improperly accumulating surplus earnings? **Two**, Has the corporation become a personal holding company?

A corporation has the right to arrange its business affairs in any (otherwise legitimate) manner that will save taxes. But the owners thereof cannot set up a corporation merely for the purpose of saving taxes. The corporation itself must be "real." That is, it must have a genuine business purpose and there must be a sound economic reason for its existence. A closely-held corporation can be disregarded by the IRS if it appears to be used solely as a means of tax avoidance. The Supreme Court so ruled in favor of the IRS to this effect way back in 1940.

In *Higgins v. Smith*, 308 US 473, the Court said—

The Government may look at actualities, and upon determining that the form employed for doing business or carrying out the challenged tax event is unreal or a sham, may sustain or disregard the effect of the fiction as best serves the purposes of the tax statute.

To prevent abuse of the C corporate form of business, a number of rather stringent federal tax rules have been enacted. The gamut runs from Section 531 through Section 537, and from Section 541 through Section 547. Illustrative of the point we are making is Section 533: *Evidence of Purpose to Avoid Income Tax*. In pertinent part, this section reads—

(a) The fact that the earnings and profits of a corporation are permitted to accumulate beyond the reasonable needs of the business shall be determinative of the purpose to avoid the income tax with respect to shareholders.

(b) The fact that any corporation is a mere holding or investment company shall be prima facie evidence of the purpose to avoid the income tax with respect to shareholders.

The significance of the above is that there is just no point in forming a C corporation for tax-only reasons. You and your associates must be driven into the corporate route by a true business necessity. Such a necessity could be for competitive reasons, protection against product and worker liabilities, and expansion plans. The most successful small C corporations are those that evolve from prior businesses operating as a partnership, an LLC, or as an S corporation.

Fiscal Year: Indefinite Life

Becoming a C corporation is easy. It is when you start operating as a corporation that you enter a new tax world.

The new world starts on the first day of the month in which you are certified as a corporation. If your certification takes place on January 29, for example, your corporate year starts on January 1. This is no different from a calendar year period for individuals.

If, instead, your certification takes place on June 29, your corporation year begins on June 1 and ends on May 31 the following year. You are now on a fiscal year accounting period. The term "fiscal year" means a period of 12 consecutive months ending on the last day of any month other than December. Most corporations operate on a fiscal year basis.

A corporation is not inhibited from adopting any fiscal year that serves its business interests. If the automatic fiscal year (commencing on date of incorporation) is not to your liking, you can elect another 12-month cycle. But you must do this very early in your startup year. To authenticate your election, you have to call a special meeting of your corporate directors and adopt a resolution setting forth the ending month of your first full fiscal year. Because of employer and other quarterly tax returns, many corporations adopt a fiscal year ending on a calendar quarter (March 31, June 30, or September 30).

When an automatic fiscal year is altered to coincide with the ending month of a calendar quarter, a *short period* corporate tax return has to be filed. If the short period is less than 45 days, a new corporation can "suspend its books" — so to speak — and file a blank Form 1120. You write across its face (in bold red letters): NO INCOME. NEW BUSINESS JUST STARTED. This action is permitted by Tax Code Section 443: short period returns for taxpayers not in existence for entire (first) taxable year.

Once your fiscal year cycle is straightened out, as a corporation, your business has indefinite life. This means that, as long as you pay the annual registration fee (to the Secretary of State of the state of incorporation), your corporate charter remains valid indefinitely. There is no preassigned or predetermined expiration date. Real corporations are formed with the intention of continuing business far into the future.

Introduction to Form 1120

Form 1120 (U.S. Corporation Income Tax Return) consists of four full pages of tax information. The four pages are partitioned into 12 subschedules totaling nearly 200 entry lines. There are over 20,000 words of official instructions for preparing Form 1120. Obviously, we cannot do full justice to this form.

Our focus is not on how to prepare Form 1120, but merely to acquaint you with it. We want to introduce some of its peculiarities. This way, you may better appreciate the comprehensiveness of Form 1120 and why corporations require so much accounting detail.

Many newly formed C corporation owners take a look at Form 1120 and literally throw up their hands. Their first reaction is: "That's not for me; that's what tax accountants are for!"

Yes, . . . perhaps.

But as an officer of the corporation, you are going to have to sign Form 1120 . . . *Under penalties of perjury.* We think you should know at least something of what you are signing.

Accordingly, we present in Figure 11.1 an outline of all the subschedules on Form 1120. We show the heading block and signature block as though all subschedules were on page 1. This, of course, is not the case. They are on four pages. Please take a moment to read through the titles of the subschedules. Then look at the very top of Figure 11.1.

We confront, now, the first peculiarity of Form 1120. There is a preprinted calendar year in bold black figures in the top right hand corner of page 1 (as is the case with all tax forms). For illustration purposes, we show the year 2006. Then, immediately below the head title, there are spaces for entering the fiscal year: *beginning _____, ending _____.* This creates a lot of confusion as to which tax year is involved.

Form 1120	**U.S. CORPORATION INCOME TAX RETURN**	**2006**
	Or tax year beginning ____ 2006, ending ____ 20___	

Business Code	*Name & Address block*	Date Incorporated

	Income	Page 1
	Deductions	
	Tax & Payments	
Schedule A	Cost of Goods Sold	Page 2
Schedule C	Dividends & Special Deductions	
Schedule E	Compensation of Officers	
Schedule J	Tax Computation & Credits	Page 3
Schedule K	Other Information	
	Capital Gains & Losses (separate Schedule D)	
Schedule L	Balance Sheets	Page 4
Schedule M-1	Reconciliation of Books With Return	
Schedule M-2	Analysis of Accumulated Earnings	

Under penalties of perjury, (etc.)

► _____ ► _____ ► _____
(Signature of Officer)   (Date)   (Title)

Fig. 11.1 - Summary Contents of a C-Corporation Tax Return

Ordinarily, one thinks of the ending year as the year for which a tax return is prepared. In the case of Form 1120, however, the preprinted calendar year signifies the **beginning** of the fiscal year. This is why the preprinted "tax year beginning" (2006 in Fig. 11.1) coincides with the tax form year (2006). Let us illustrate.

Suppose your fiscal year begins July 1, 2006 and ends June 30, 2007. Which preprinted calendar year tax form do you use: 2006 or 2007? What does the IRS computer "see"?

Answer: 2006 — the year in which your fiscal year *begins.*

Administratively, there is a reason for this filing-year anomaly for C corporations. In our example above, the 2007 tax forms are not government printed until very late in 2006 or early in 2007. For fiscal years ending in March, June, or September of 2007, no 2007 tax forms would be available. Hence, the 2006 already printed forms have to be used.

We are calling your attention to this anomaly because it is NOT a trivial matter. Today, the IRS is terribly automated and computerized. If you try using ending year common sense, and use the wrong preprinted-year tax forms, you will be computer terrorized. There will be endless IRS computer mismatching problems. So, do take heed. Use the computer consistent preprinted-year tax forms.

Income & Deduction Items

The profit and loss aspects of a C corporation are comparable to those of every other for-profit trade or business. This is because the income and deductions subschedules are strikingly similar. It is a pure business accounting matter.

Proprietorships, partnerships, LLCs, and S corporations have multiple sources of income against which prioritized deductions are allowed. The key difference is the net income (or loss) after deductions. For C corporations, the net income (profit) is *taxable income* . . . now! The amount of tax is computed elsewhere on Form 1120, and then entered immediately below the taxable income line on page 1 as **Total tax**. Against this amount, offsets are allowed for prepayments and applicable credits.

If there is a net loss on Form 1120, it is not taxable. It rides on the books as a *net operating loss* (NOL). For new startup corporations, the NOL can be carried forward as another deduction for the following year. It does not pass through to the owners in any way. An NOL denies any dividends to the shareholders.

Before touching on a few other points, we should present Figure 11.2. We do so on the next page.

Form 1120	CORPORATION INCOME TAX RETURN	TAX YEAR
Income		**Amount**
1	Gross receipts (less returns & allowances)	
2	Cost of goods sold	
3	Gross profit (subtract line 2 from line 1)	
4	Gross dividends (Schedule C)	
5	Gross interest	
6	Gross rents	
7	Gross royalties	
8	Net capital gain (Schedule D)	
9	Other net gain or loss (Form 4797)	
10	Other income (attach statement)	
11	//////////// TOTAL INCOME ▶	
Deductions		**Amount**
12	Compensation of officers (Schedule E)	
13	Salaries & wages (other than officers)	
14	Repairs	
15	Bad debts (specific write-offs)	
16	Rents	
17	Taxes (other than income taxes)	
18	Interest	
19	Contributions (max. 10% of taxable income)	
20	Depreciation (Form 4562)	
21	Amortization (Form 4562)	
22	Depletion	
23	Advertising	
24	Pension & profit sharing plans	
25	Employee benefit programs	
26	Other deductions (attach statement)	
27	//////////// TOTAL DEDUCTIONS ▶	
28	Taxable Income - Tentative ▶ ▶ ▶	
29	LESS Special Deductions	//////////
	a. Net Operating Loss (attach statement)	
	b. Dividends Deduction (Schedule C)	
30	TAXABLE INCOME - Net ▶ ▶ ▶ ▶ ▶	

Fig. 11.2 - Sequence to Taxable Income on Form 1120

Editorial Note: Item 26 can be as many as 15 to 25 other items.

Figure 11.2 is a slightly edited version of the income and deduction lines on Form 1120. You might note that there are 10 income lines and 15 deduction lines.

One of the first items to particularly note in Figure 11.2 is the *Gross dividends* income line. It is accompanied by the parenthetical instruction: "Schedule C." Do not confuse this Schedule C with the Schedule C (Form 1040) of a proprietorship. Schedule C (Form 1120) serves a totally different purpose (as will be discussed shortly below).

Another income item to note on Form 1120 is *Net capital gain.* This is the gain derived from the sale of capital assets of the corporation (not of goods or services). Interestingly, there is no income line provision for net capital loss. What happens if there is a net capital loss for the year?

The net capital loss of a C corporation is carried back three years to combine with any capital gain for those years. If there is no prior capital gain, the net capital loss is carried forward for five years to combine with any likely capital gain for those years.

Are you beginning to sense the different machinations of C corporation's tax accounting?

On the deductions side of the ledger, there is the treatment of owner salaries. If a shareholder in a corporation is also an officer of that corporation, he/she must be paid a salary. The salaries of all owner-officers are displayed on a separate subschedule (Schedule E) on Form 1120. Each officer's name, social security number, percentage of time devoted to business, percentage of stock ownership, and amount of compensation are shown. All compensation to officers is deductible against the income of the corporation. Other than magnitude, there is no deduction difference for other employees.

On Form 1120, when the total deductions are subtracted from total income, the taxable income at that point is a *tentative* amount. We so indicated this at line 28 in Figure 11.2. Against this tentative taxable income, there are two entirely new deductions. These two deductions are—

(a) The NOL deduction (carryover or carryback)

(b) Special deductions (Schedule C)

When these two deductions are subtracted from the tentative taxable income, the net becomes the taxable income.

Generally, a C corporation may carry an NOL back to each of two years preceding the year of the loss, and carry it over to each of 20 years following the year of the loss (Sec. 172(b)). There are deviations from this general rule for product liability losses, disaster losses, and farming losses. When claiming an NOL deduction, a comprehensive carryback-carryforward statement of computations must be attached to Form 1120.

Schedule C (1120): Uniquely Special

On two occasions above, there was mention of "Schedule C" (Form 1120). In Figure 11.1 we identified this subschedule as *Dividends and Special Deductions.* This is a class of deductions that applies only to C corporations **receiving** dividends from other C corporations. The deduction theory is based on the fact that the "other corporation" dividends have already been taxed.

These special dividend deductions are prescribed by Sections 243 through 247 of the tax code. They are pronounced "shall be allowed" by Section 241: *Allowance of Special Deductions for Corporations.* This section reads in part as—

> *In addition to the deductions provided* [elsewhere]*, there shall be allowed as deductions in computing taxable income the items specified in this part.*

The tax code phrase "this part" refers to the following sections (among others):

Sec. 243 — Dividends Received from Domestic Corporations
Sec. 244 — Dividends Received on Certain Preferred Stock
Sec. 245 — Dividends Received from Foreign Corporations
Sec. 246 — Dividends from Debt Financed Stock
Sec. 247 — Dividends from Preferred Stock of Public Utilities

All of this dividend income to a corporation is subject to a deduction varying from 40% to 100%. The 100% deduction applies to affiliated corporations and wholly-owned subsidiaries.

Otherwise, the deduction is scaled from 40% to 80% depending on the extent of ownership in other corporate entities.

This special dividend deduction tempts many small corporations to invest heavily into large domestic, foreign, and public utility corporations. In some cases, this temptation is the sole motivating factor for incorporating versus not incorporating.

Caution. There is a tax trap here for you. Ask yourself: "What happens to the 40% to 100% of untaxed dividend income that is corporatively received?"

Answer: The untaxed dividends are passed through to the owner-officers as salaries, or declared as dividends to all shareholders. In either case, they are subject to ordinary income tax by the individual recipients. Surely you did not think that 40% to 100% of your corporate income as dividends received would never be taxed, did you?

In reality, small C corporations just starting up are unable to take advantage of the special deductions in Schedule C (1120). Most startup businesses tend to be undercapitalized. Rarely is there excess capital available to invest in large corporations that pay attractive dividends.

Tax Computation Complex

Schedule J (1120) is titled: *Tax Computation*. It appears on page 3 (upper portion) of Form 1120. It consists of 12 checkboxes, 16 entry lines, and about 3,000 words of instructions. It is not a simple computational process by any means. It is much more than a matter of using the taxable income on page 1 and correlating said amount with an 8-step schedule of graduated rates.

The sequence of computational events on Schedule J (1120) goes like this—

1. Regular income tax (at graduated rates) .... _____

2. Controlled group tax (plus 5% surtax) .... _____

3. PSC (personal service) tax (flat 35% in lieu of regular) .... _____

4. AMT (alternative minimum) tax (Form 4626) .... _____

5. Tentative tax (Add 1, 2, 3, and 4)...................._____

6. Total credits allowed (up to 25 potential)..........< _____ >

7. Reduced tax (Subtract 6 from 5)......................._____

8. PHC (personal holding) tax (a flat 35% rate)......_____

9. Other taxes (4 possible)................................._____

10. **Total tax** (Add 7, 8, and 9)........................ ►_____

Unless there is zero or negative taxable income, at least one of these taxes will apply. In some (rare) cases, all may apply *simultaneously*! So, if you are going to incorporate for tax-saving reasons, you had better think again.

The regular corporate tax is based on a graduated rate schedule. The lowest rate is 15% on taxable incomes up to $50,000. For taxable incomes over $10,000,000 ($10 million), the rate goes to 35% . . . plus an "additional tax" of 5%. When the tax is computed, it is entered on the *Income tax* line on Schedule J.

The corporate minimum tax is an "alternate" tax designed to defeat the extensive use of "tax preferences." Tax preference deductions include accelerated depreciation, certain amortization and depletion, installment sales, research expenditures, environmental matters, bad debt loss reserves, and "excess book income." The tax is 25% of the preference deductions that exceed $150,000 and 20% if they exceed $310,000. The minimum tax is computed by using Form 4626 *Alternative Minimum Tax—Corporations*. Form 4626 is then attached to Form 1120.

The letters "PSC" above stand for: *Personal Service Corporation*. Such an entity is one that performs substantially all activities . . . *in the fields of health, law, engineering, architecture, accounting, actuarial science, performing arts, or consulting.* Additionally, the letters "PHC" stand for: *Personal Holding Company*. The PHC tax applies when 60% or more of the corporation's income is derived from such passive sources as interest, dividends, rents, royalties, and the like. The PSC and PHC tax rate is a flat 35%. It is computed separately as PSC or PHC on Schedule PH (1120).

The "controlled group tax" above is a surtax on a parent company which owns 80% or more of the stock in one or more subsidiary corporations. The use of subsidiary corporations is often a tax dilution tactic by the controlling interests (those holding more than 50% of the voting power) in the parent corporation.

There is one area in which a C corporation has a slight tax edge over other core business forms. This is in the area of tax credits. A "credit" is a dollar-for-dollar offset (subtraction) against the computed tax. It is not that the credits are designed to favor C corporations (the credits are available to all forms of business), it is just that, with greater amounts of money available, a C corporation can engage in a greater diversity of activities where the credits are applicable. Even small C corporations can grow big.

There are about 25 types of tax credits available in the federal tax code. To claim any of these credits, a separately designated tax form for each type of credit is required. If you claimed 10 different tax credits, for example, you'd have to attach 10 different credit forms to Schedule J (1120). Corporate tax credits are never automatic. If you are eligible for any of them, you must stake your claim with the proper form.

Balance Sheet Features

All filers of Form 1120 should complete Schedule L: *Balance Sheets*. For those whose total receipts *and* total assets are $250,000 or more, Schedule L **must** be completed. This schedule constitutes a financial statement of the corporate entity for each fiscal year. It is very comprehensive.

Because of its basic importance to corporate tax accounting, we present in Figure 11.3 a near replica of the line items on Schedule L (on page 4 of Form 1120). For space reasons, we have abridged the entry columns. Otherwise, the line items and the sequence numbering are correct. We are doing this because we want to point out a few items that are novel to C corporations.

Small, closely-held C corporations tend to engage — indiscriminately — in personal loans back and forth between the corporation and its stockholders. The loans tend to be at below market rates of interest or at no interest at all. Also, the loans tend not to be properly documented. Often, the loans are just penciled book entries that are erased on the verbal say of the principal owners (those holding more than 50% of the voting stock).

Schedule L	BALANCE SHEETS	Form 1120 - Page 4		
			Beginning of year	End of year
Assets				
1	Cash on hand			
2	Trade notes & accounts receivable			
	a. Less allowance for bad debts		< >	
3	Inventories			
4	Federal & state government obligations			
5	Other current assets (attach schedule)			
6	Loans TO stockholders			
7	Mortgage & real estate loans			
8	Other investments (attach schedule)			
9	Buildings & other depreciable assets			
	a. Less accumulated depreciation		< >	
10	Depletable assets			
	a. Less accumulated depletion		< >	
11	Land (net of any amortization)			
12	Intangible assets (amortizable only)			
	a. Less accumulated amortization		< >	
13	Other assets (attach schedule)			
14	**TOTAL ASSETS** ▶ ▶ ▶ ▶ ▶				
Liabilities				
15	Accounts payable			
16	Notes payable in less than 1 year			
17	Other current liabilities (attach schedule)			
18	Loans FROM stockholders			
19	Notes payable in 1 year or more			
20	Other liabilities (attach schedule)			
21	Capital stock: a. Preferred Stock			
	b. Common Stock			
22	Paid-in or capital surplus			
23	Retained earnings - appropriated			
24	Retained earnings - unappropriated			
25	Less cost of treasury stock			< >
26	**TOTAL LIABILITIES** ▶ ▶ ▶ ▶ ▶				
> > > > > > > > > > > > > and stock holders equity				

Fig. 11.3 - Items Listed on Form 1120 Balance Sheets

Editorial Note: Treasury stock, item 25, is the buy back of stock previously sold. It is available for resale or cancellation.

To prevent excessive looseness in stockholder loans accounting, Schedule L (1120) requires recordation of these loans at items 6 (TO stockholders) and 18 (FROM stockholders) . . . in Figure 11.3. These loans have to be accounted for. Furthermore, *applicable federal rates of interest* must be used (IRC Sec. 7872). If not timely used, the IRS can apply these rates retroactively to all stockholder loans made after June 6, 1984.

At item 22 (in Fig. 11.3) the entry reads: *Paid-in or capital surplus.* This, in effect, is the current book value of corporate stock in excess of its value at time of issue (item 21). This "surplus" is the unrealized portion of capital gain not identified elsewhere on Schedule L. This surplus derives from the appreciation in corporate property values and the increasing net worth of the business. This is a "balancing entry" that changes from year to year. In contrast, item 21 remains fixed.

At items 23 and 24, the entries read respectively: *Retained earnings — Appropriated/Unappropriated.* Retained earnings are those profits in a corporation that have **not** been distributed to stockholders as dividends. "Appropriated" retained earnings are those that are earmarked for specific spending plans of the business, such as for new equipment, new buildings, new markets.

"Unappropriated" retained earnings are excess money floating around in the corporation with no earmarked business purpose in mind. This money is called *accumulated earnings.* This money comes under the watchful eye of the IRS. If more than $250,000, it is subject to a 15% penalty tax. The purpose of this penalty is to arm-twist corporate directors into distributing these earnings to individual stockholders where it can be income taxed to them.

We have not done justice to a C corporation. Its potential is far beyond that which we have addressed as a less than $10,000,000 ($10 million) enterprise. When total assets exceed this level, a **Schedule M-3** (Form 1120) is required. The M-3 focuses on global corporations with multiple associated entities issuing publicly traded stock that has been registered with the U.S. Securities and Exchange Commission (in Washington, D.C.). Because our focus is strictly on "small" C corporations, we have purposely bypassed Schedule M-3.

As a summary and check-list, other advantages and dis-advantages of a C corporation are presented in Figure 11.4. There is one very practical feature of a C corporation. It can be sold or redeemed in parts and pieces (shares), without disrupting the continuity of the business. On the other hand, if the business fails, you cannot close the doors and walk away. The corporation has to be legally dissolved. This takes time . . . and more money.

C CORPORATION		
ADVANTAGES		**DISADVANTAGES**
1.	Has potential access to substantial amounts of "other people's money"; 5 to 35 stockholders practical for "small" corporation; no upper limit imposed.	1. Legal registration of stock may be required; capitalization fees imposed; not practical if gross annual sales less than $250,000.
2.	Board of directors appoints principal operating officers; officers can be changed without jeopardizing policies, objectives, & operating staff.	2. Director's "minutes" required; written policies & procedures required; salaries & perks "highly concentrated" at the top; invites tax attack.
3.	Has potential of "indefinite life"; this fosters long range marketing plans & new product development; attracts new venture capital & causes business to grow.	3. If business unsuccessful, cannot simply "walk away"; product liabilities and service warranties must be honored; attracts lawsuits & high "damage awards".
4.	Except if "closely-held", stockholders are not active participants; this frees management to devote its "best effort" towards success of business.	4. All tax, accounting, & financial affairs far more complex; officer-owners often mix personal interest with corporate interests; travel & entertainment rise.
5.	A more acceptable form of business for intra-state, interstate, & international trade; growth "potentially" unlimited.	5. As markets expand, so do all the problems; internal corruption & bureaucracy grow; necessitates greater expertise of personnel.
6.	More attractive to high calibre employees seeking careers & professional development; also fosters "spin-off" businesses.	6. Employees want pay raises, bonuses, fringe benefits, pension & profit sharing plans; overhead costs mount & get out of hand.

Fig. 11.4 - Other Pros and Cons of a C Corporation

12

COMPENSATION OF OWNERS

> Because Of Ownership Control And Self-Interest, An Owner's Compensatory Forms Are More Closely Tax Scrutinized Than Nonowner Employees. Business Meals, Entertainment, And Vacations Are Virtually "No-No." Most Owner Benefits Must Be NON-DISCRIMINATORY With Respect To Employees. When Employing One's Spouse And Children, Their Training And Capabilities Must Be Matched To Actual Services Performed. By A Combination Of Pension, Profit-Sharing, And Deferred Compensation Plans, As Much as $40,000 Can Be "Trusteed" Away Each Year For An Owner's Own Old Age And Retirement.

As reward for their efforts, the owners of a business want to know two things. One: "How much money can I pull out of the business for myself?" Two: "How can I pay the minimum tax on the money I draw?"

The answer to the first question depends on the form of business and the degree of its success. The answer to the second question depends on taking advantage of: (a) "safe" fringe benefits, (b) family dilution techniques, and (c) pension and profit-sharing plans.

We have purposely framed these two questions and answers. We have done this so as to focus this chapter on the relationship between the owner (or owners) and his/her/their business. After all, the purpose in starting one's business (in addition to a livelihood) is to make money and keep as much of that money as possible for one's self. Human self-interest is central to the profit motivation for starting any business.

Very few persons — no matter how upright they may be as citizens — go into business simply to generate tax revenue for government. Such revenue is strictly a by-product. The underlying purpose of any business is to generate money for the enjoyment of life, and to prepare for one's old age and retirement. All of this is what we mean by "compensation of owners."

Owners Are "Naturally Suspect"

Owners of a business, regardless of its form, are natural targets for tax suspicion. This is because owners control the business: its income, its assets, and its expenditures. The owners are the ones taking the risk. Because so, they have the greatest self-interest at stake. The IRS deliberately targets this self-interest.

Consequently, in the processing of tax returns, an owner's return is screened more closely than a nonowner's return. The screening focuses primarily on the adequacy of personal income reported, and on the extent of personal benefit expenditures claimed. There is a perpetual undercurrent of bureaucracy suspicion that an owner is "trying to get away with something."

All tax returns are "profiled" and classified before they go through the IRS screening process. This way, the screeners — both human and electronic — concentrate on selected items and "measure" them against quantitative standards. These are probability tests developed over years of screening profiled returns for additional revenue.

If a business owner's return is selected for examination, there is an additional personal questionnaire involved. This is Form 8422: *Statement of Annual Estimated Personal and Family Expenses.* Some 35 preprinted entry lines are involved, plus blank lines for the hand entry of other items that a revenue agent may be curious about. The tax presumption behind Form 4822 is that, somehow, you are "skimming the business." You are using the business to pay for personal and family expenses.

Typical of such presumed skimming items are personal and family expenditures for—

- Barber, beauty shop, & cosmetics
- Clothing, laundry, & dry cleaning
- Furniture, appliances, & fixtures
- Home repairs & improvements
- Recreation, entertainment, & vacations

If you object too confrontationally to this invasion of your privacy and presumption of innocence, Section 262 of the tax code may be cited to you. This section reads—

Except as otherwise provided, no deduction shall be allowed for personal, living, or family expenses.

Regulation 1.262-1 amplifies on this wording. It gives the impression that the IRS can search your entire home and frisk all members of your family.

You can — and should — refuse to comply with Form 4822. Do this on the grounds that Section 262 is positioned in the tax code under Subchapter B (Taxable Income), Part IX: ITEMS NOT DEDUCTIBLE. Therefore, you can take the stance that, if you are not claiming these items on your personal or business tax returns, the IRS is out of order in asking for them. But, do be sure that you definitely are not claiming them as deductible expenses.

Limit "Meals & Entertainment"

Every business owner has a universal desire. He wants to build up the goodwill of the business in the hope that it will grow and prosper. The ordinary "tools" for this are business meals, small gifts, and social entertainment. Every business does it . . . more or less. But, if the owner of a business himself participates in the goodwill expenditures, said expenses are carefully scrutinized.

Because travel, meals, and entertainment (TME) expenses will be scrutinized mercilessly, we suggest that as an owner you pursue a policy of limited participation in business meals and entertainment. You may allow these for your employees and nonemployees (provided they submit documented expense vouchers to you), but limit them for yourself. Travel on business (away from home overnight) is another matter. Compared to meals, gifts, and entertainment, business travel is more conveniently documented. Besides, extensive travel by small business owners is not all that frequent.

The principal reason we urge limiting your meals and entertainment (M&E) is Section 274: *Disallowance of Certain Entertainment, Etc., Expenses.* This tax rule targets gifts, entertainment, amusement, vacation, recreation, cruise ships, food, beverages, sports tickets, and so on. As an owner of a business, if you participate in these affairs, you will be "beaten over the head" with Section 274. Revenue agents are taught to believe that no business is M&E clean.

Section 274 consists of 15 subsections comprising approximately 5,000 words. Its basic thrust is in subsection 274(d): *Substantiation Required.* This subsection reads in part—

No deduction or credit shall be allowed . . . unless the taxpayer substantiates by adequate records or by sufficient evidence corroborating—

(A) the amount of such expense or other item,
(B) the [date], time and place [involved],
(C) the business purpose of the expense or other item,
(D) the business relationship to the taxpayer of persons entertained, using the facility or property, or receiving the gift.

Even after documenting all M&E, only 50% is deductible [Sec. 274(n)]! This is so whether you or your business picks up the tab.

In short, as owner of a business, discipline yourself against "wining and dining" at the expense of your business. The opportunities that you've heard of in the past are gone now. You are expected to absorb certain "no-no" benefits because there are other statutory benefits which are "safe."

Nondiscriminatory Insurance Plans

Although M&E expenditures are scrutinized mercilessly, there are a number of other benefits that are quite acceptable . . . and nontaxable. An overview of these safe benefits is presented in Figure 12.1 Foremost are certain insurance plans.

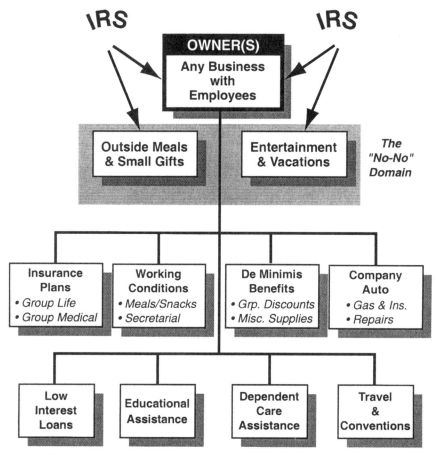

Fig. 12.1 - Nontaxable Owner Benefits (Compensation Related)

Many businesses, large as well as small, offer various insurance plans to their owners and employees. This is done to take advantage of group rates, as well as to assure piece of mind during employment. Some of the plans are statutorily acceptable; some are not. The acceptable ones are those that are characterized as *nondiscriminatory.* Nondiscriminatory plans do not substantially favor owners at the expense of employees.

Company-paid insurance plans are in the form of compensation that, ordinarily, would be includible in the recipient's gross income. However, there are two types of insurance that are statutorily recognized as *exclusions from income.* These two types and their sections of the tax code are:

1. Group-term life insurance   [Sec. 79]
2. Group accident and health   [Sec. 106]

Section 79 (Group-Term Life Insurance Purchased for Employees) allows an employer to pay premiums on policies with face values up to $50,000 without requiring those premiums to be reported as income to the employee. For coverage in excess of $50,000, the excess premiums are reported as income on each employee's Form W-2. The "catch" here is that the insured person must be an **employee**. This rules out self-employed owners of proprietorships and some partnerships. Otherwise, the premiums paid are deductible by the business.

Section 106 (Contributions by Employer to Accident and Health Plans) also permits the business to pay the premiums (as deductible expenses) without reporting the premiums as income to the employee. If the plan is nondiscriminatory and provides continuous coverage, the owners (as active participants in the business) may also be covered. On this point, Section 106(a) specifically says—

Gross income of an employee does not include employer-provided coverage under an accident or health plan.

But, again, only employees (including owner-employees) are benefited. All other insurance plans paid for by the business must be related directly and specifically to the business itself. There can be no spillover of benefits whatsoever to the owners, be they owner-employees or self-employeds. This is particularly true for "key person" insurance, disability insurance, hazard insurance, liability insurance, and performance insurance. As an owner, don't let yourself ever succumb to the temptation to include in your business insurance programs coverage for homeowner's insurance, personal auto insurance, and flight insurance for family vacations.

Business-necessitated insurance is referred to as "Section 162 plans" (ordinary and necessary business expenses).

"Safe Harbor" Benefits

There are at least five other statutory areas where owners (as active participants) may derive "compensation related" benefits which are tax free. The catch, again, is that the programs must be nondiscriminatory and they should be in writing. If these and other conditions are met, payments for the benefits are deductible expenses to the business. Furthermore, the business cost of the benefits is not includible in the gross income of the recipients (be they owners, officers, employees, or nonemployees). We call these "safe harbor" benefits because they are expressly authorized in the Internal Revenue Code. There are also pertinent IRS regulations on each benefit and its limitations.

The five particular benefits that we have in mind are—

(1) Sec. 119 — Meals served on business premises
(2) Sec. 127 — Up to $5,250 in "educational assistance"
(3) Sec. 129 — Up to $5,000 for "dependent care"
(4) Sec. 132 — "Working condition" fringes
(5) Sec. 7872 — Up to $10,000 interest-free loans

A word or two on each of these statutory benefits is instructive.

Section 119 says, in essence, that if meals are served on business premises for business reasons, and are paid for by the business, they are not taxable benefits to the meal recipients. Many small businesses have designated areas where food (packaged or catered), snacks, and beverages can be consumed. An owner is not disbarred from having business meals on his own premises. If an owner normally stays at his place of business after hours, meals served during those hours also would qualify. This could be opportunity to offset some of the (previously mentioned) owner-absorbed meals and entertainment consumed off-premises.

Section 127 permits a business to pay for tuition, books, supplies, and tools (up to $5,250) for instruction that improves or develops the capabilities of an employee. The only requirement is that instruction be at an educational institution, and that the course(s) **not** be in sports, games, hobbies, or recreational activities. The curriculum must have academic overtones.

Section 129 permits a business to pay up to $5,000 in "assistance" to an employee for the care of a child, incapacitated spouse, or elderly parent . . . while the employee is at work.

Section 132 addresses "working condition" and "de minimis" fringes. These are incidental benefits that are part of the everyday working environment of each particular type of business. The direct cost of these benefits is obscure and is generally part of the ordinary business operation (employee discounts, for example).

Section 7872 (Treatment of Loans with Below-Market Interest Rates) is probably more directed at owners rather than employees. Compensation-related loans up to $10,000 may be interest free. For loans up to $100,000 the interest must equal the "net investment income" from such loans. For loans in excess of $100,000, the interest must be imputed at the "applicable federal rate." These are called *gift loans* because no collateral, security, or qualifying (personal) financial statements are required. The thrust of Section 7872 is that an owner borrowing money from his own business is acceptable, so long as the interest rules are followed and there is written documentation on each loan.

A "Company-Provided" Auto

Every owner of a business needs a car for business purposes. It is virtually impossible to conduct any business today by remaining on business premises all day long, every day, without ever leaving to attend to some business matter. Consequently, a business car is a "working condition" necessity [Sec. 132(a)(3)].

The question in every owner's mind is: "How can the business provide a car for my use, with the least recordkeeping fuss and bother . . . and beyond scrutiny by the IRS?"

Basically, every company-provided auto is a taxable fringe benefit. The taxable portion is the personal use of the car: not its business use. The taxable portion is satisfied in one of two ways. It is treated either as—

(a) compensation to the owner (by the business), which is reported as income on his personal return, or

(b) reimbursement to the business (by the owner), which is reported as income on the business return.

For overall simplicity in recordkeeping, the compensation treatment is preferred. The owner is taxed on a relatively minor amount, whereas the business gets a 100% writeoff for all expenses of operating the vehicle. There are two compensation reporting methods, namely:

(a) "commute only" with a utility type auto, and
(b) "annual lease" of a luxury type auto

In the "commute only" method, the business buys a utility car (say, a $15,000 vehicle) and assigns it to the owner. A written contract is prepared that prohibits the car from being used for personal purposes other than commuting between home and business. The contract also requires that the owner have a personal vehicle of his own, for family and vacation use. If these conditions are met, the business reports $3 per commute day as additional taxable income to the owner. Typically, this would be $750 per year (for 250 commute days).

In the "annual lease" method, the business buys or leases a luxury car (say, a $35,000 vehicle) and assigns it to the owner. The owner is allowed to use the car for other than commuting. However, he must report to the business each year his true percentage of personal use of the vehicle. Say this personal use is 25%. Based on IRS tables, the annual lease value of a $35,000 auto is $9,250. At 25% personal use, the amount of $2,313 per year ($9,250 x 25%) would be reported by the business as additional income to the owner.

In both methods (commute only and annual lease), the business deducts 100% of all operating expenses on the vehicle. For convenience in this regard, many businesses obtain gas and repair credit cards and assign them to the drivers of each company-provided vehicle. This, in itself, is a significant tax benefit to the business owner(s).

Livelihood Compensation Differences

All of the foregoing (nontaxable) benefits are classed as *nonlivelihood* compensation. Except for the small taxable portions that we have identified, all expenditures therewith are fully deductible by the business. This is true whether the business is a proprietorship, an LLC, a partnership, an S corporation, or a C corporation. The only requirement is that the business has employees in addition to the participating owners themselves. A business with owners only would be hard pressed to qualify for nondiscriminatory benefits.

When we get into livelihood compensation, the form in which a business is conducted does make a difference. Except in the corporate form, the participating owners are not employees. Their livelihood depends on the net profit or loss of the business. The differences in livelihood compensation for the different forms of business are summarized in Figure 12.2. As self-evident therein, at the "bottom line" all such compensation is fully taxable.

In a sole proprietorship, the owner's livelihood compensation is simply the net earnings from the business. The true amount of his net earnings is not known until the end of the taxable year. Aside from using personal credit cards, what does a proprietor do for livelihood purposes during the intervening 12 months?

Answer: He makes an "anticipatory draw" from time to time throughout the year. Even if he does not need to do this for livelihood reasons (assuming he lived off of his savings), he would have to do it for estimated tax *prepayment* purposes. The owner of a proprietorship is not on a regular salary; therefore, he is not subject to periodic withholdings. But he is subject to mandatory prepayments of his tax. He makes these prepayments on quarterly voucher forms 1040-ES.

In an LLC arrangement, as well as in a general partnership, each participant's livelihood compensation is his "distributive share" of the net earnings of the business. Similarly to a proprietorship, the LLC members and general partners are not on a salary. They can, however, receive "guaranteed payments." They can use these payments, if not for livelihood, for their estimated tax prepayments. If the partnership engages bona fide employees, the guaranteed payments to partners could be structured as wages, subject to all withholdings.

In an S corporation or a C corporation, the owners — as officers/employees — draw a "stipulated salary" for their livelihood compensation. They can do this in anticipation of the corporate net profit for the year. Or, as many closely-held corporations do, the owners agree to a nominal salary for the year, and then assign themselves a *bonus* at the end of the year, when the profit picture is better known. The salary and bonus are subject to full withholdings for both income and social security/medicare taxes. Recall Chapter 4 in this regard.

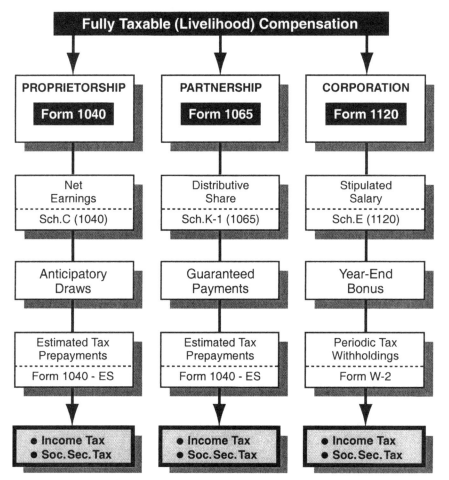

Fig. 12.2 - The Livelihood Compensation of Business Owners

Any year-end bonus must be based on the individual productivity of the owners and *not* on the number of shares that each holds. Any bonus based on ownership share will be tax treated as *dividends.* A dividend is not a deductible expense of the corporation, whereas a bonus is deductible. A bonus is compensation for personal services, whereas a dividend is compensation for capital invested. A dividend is income taxed twice: once at the corporate level and again at the individual shareholder level. A dividend, however, is not subject to social security and medicare tax, whereas a bonus is so taxed.

Employing Spouse & Children

In successful businesses the practice often is to employ family members — particularly the spouse and children — of the owner(s). This is good practice where there is genuine business need for the training, experience, and capabilities of selected family members. Actual services must be performed, and the compensation must be reasonable. Here, the term "reasonable" means comparable to that paid to nonfamily employees for the same tasks being performed.

There must be a bona fide employer-employee relationship between each owner and his/her spouse and children. If such relationship exists, there can be some tax *dilution* benefits to the owner. But one has to be certain that the dilution is genuine. It cannot be a disguise for personal expenses, family chores, children's education, or gifts to minors.

When employing one's spouse in a business, there is virtually no income tax dilution. Most married persons file joint returns. Consequently, any diminution of the owner's income by the amount paid to his spouse is simply added back into the joint gross income. The key benefits with spousal employees are the social security/medicare tax and retirement plan deductions.

Ordinarily, when starting a business, one "employs" his (or her) spouse on a noncompensatory basis. That is, the spouse helps out doing odd jobs, part time. But, as the business gets going, the spouse may want a separate social security/medicare base of her (or his) own. If so, the spouse can be treated as an "independent contractor" in a proprietorship, an "associate partner" in a partnership, an "active member" in an LLC, or as a "regular employee" in a corporation. However treated, there is social security/medicare tax on the spousal earnings.

Regardless of the form of business, an employed spouse can become a participant in an employer-sponsored retirement plan. This, in effect, becomes additional deferred compensation that may be tax beneficial to an owner.

When it comes to employing dependent children of the owner(s) of a business, there are real skepticism and challenge by the IRS. Do the children perform useful productive services for the business? Or, are they performing parental-directed chores that they would be expected to do, whether the parent(s) owned the business or not? Is their compensation just enough to offset other child-rearing costs such as education, tutoring, recreation, sports activities? Do the children file income tax returns?

For years after 1986, employed (dependent) children's tax returns become rather complex. Each child's income has to be distinguished between "unearned" and "earned." Unearned income by children under 14 is subject to the parent's tax rate. Earned income is subject to the child's tax rate. Children under 18 employed in a parent's business are exempt from social security/medicare tax.

Nondependent children (18 and over) file their own tax returns like any other young adult. The only difference is that, if they are employed by a parent while being a full-time student away from home, there is a serious question whether any bona fide business services have been performed.

In all cases of minor and young adult children being employed by parents, *time sheets* become a requisite for documenting the actual services performed. And, of course, all employed children must use their own social security numbers.

Qualified Retirement Plans

One of the true tax benefits of owning a business is owner participation in one or more qualified retirement plans. A "qualified" plan is one that is tax qualified under the latest rules that are applicable. A business can make certain contributions to each plan and simultaneously write off those contributions as a deductible expense of the business. Such contributions are *not* included in the gross income of the owner. In addition, an owner may make limited contributions on his own, and get an immediate tax deduction for his contributions (so long as the plan is "tax qualified"). Be aware, however, that the contributions **are** subject to social security/medicare tax withholdings and matchings.

The feature that makes retirement plans tax attractive is the establishment of an *employee trust* for each plan. Each trust is a legal entity, somewhat like that of a corporation. It differs in that it is a tax exempt entity. It is tax exempt by virtue of the fact that all corpus (contributions and assets) and income are reserved for the exclusive benefit of the plan participants. The reserved money is not taxed until it is withdrawn from the trust by the contributor participant or by his designated survivor.

All qualified plans — whether pension, profit-sharing, stock bonus, deferred compensation, or other — must meet certain stringent statutory conditions. These conditions are spelled out in Sections 401 through 417 of the Internal Revenue Code. Altogether, these sections encompass approximately 90,000 words of text. Yes — 90,000 words! Section 401 alone covers some 14,000 words. Subsection 401(a), **Requirements for Qualification**, is the key introduction to all retirement plans.

The leadoff wording in Section 401(a) reads in part as—

A trust created or organized in the United States and forming part of a stock bonus, pension, or profit-sharing plan of an employer for the exclusive benefit of his employees or their beneficiaries shall constitute a qualified trust . . .

> *(1) If contributions are made to the trust by such employer, or employees, or both . . .*
> *(2) If under the trust instrument it is impossible . . . for any part of the corpus or income to be . . . used for, or diverted to, purposes other than for the exclusive benefit of his employees or their beneficiaries . . .*
> *(3) If the plan of which such trust is a part satisfies the . . . minimum participation standards, and*
> *(4) If the contributions or benefits provided under the plan do not discriminate in favor of employees who are:*
>> *(A) officers,*
>> *(B) shareholders, or*
>> *(C) highly compensated.*

Altogether, there are some 25 or so requirements for qualifying a retirement plan as a tax-exempt trust. Obviously, we cannot even begin to discuss the requirements. But we can pictorialize them, as we have done in Figure 12.3. Our Figure 12.3 at least should convey the idea that another tax accountable — yet, tax deferred — entity has to be set up, administered, and maintained.

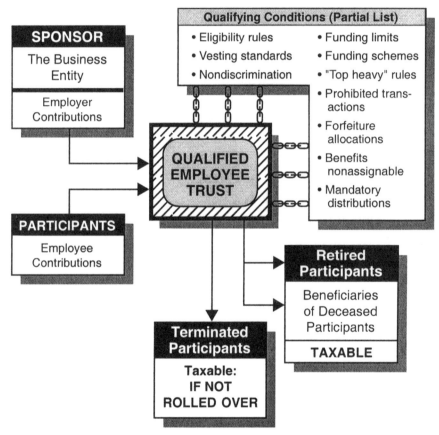

Fig. 12.3 - Features of a Business-Sponsored Retirement Plan

Any small business owner can set up his own retirement trust(s), so long as he provides proportionately for all nonowner employees. He can do this by adopting one or more "standardized form plans" made available by a sponsoring organization that already has received IRS approval. Various financial institutions offer these standardized plans. Most such plans have adequate flexibility for investing the retirement contributions in a prudent and conservative manner.

Annual Contribution Limits

Every business owner wants to contribute the maximum possible amount of money to his own retirement. But there are certain overall limits. For one, the maximum "compensation base" that can be taken into account is "about" $200,000 per year. (The "about" refers to annual cost-of-living adjustments.) All retirement plans, in one way or another, are keyed to a participant's compensation for services rendered. This applies to owner-employees as well as to nonowner employees. For retirement plan purposes, all participating owners are automatically classed as owner-employees, regardless of the form of business.

In the past, one of the schemes that owners used was to "long-rig" the vesting schedules of their company's retirement plans. A vesting schedule is the length of time — typically 3 to 7 years — that is required before a nonowner participant is 100% vested. If an employee were terminated short of his full vesting period, some of the employer's contributions on behalf of that employee would be forfeited. The forfeited contributions had the effect of increasing the owner's retirement benefits. Owners usually set the vesting schedules to coincide with their own interests. This is no longer possible. Today, all nonowner forfeitures are treated as employer contributions, subject to an annual limitation amount.

As per Section 415(c), the *annual addition* to a retirement plan is the sum of:

(A) employer contributions,
(B) employee contributions, and
(C) forfeitures.

The annual addition to a defined *contribution* plan cannot exceed **the lesser of**:

(a) $40,000 or
(b) 25 percent of the participant's compensation.

This means that, if an employee contributes nothing, and if there are no forfeitures, an employer can contribute up to $40,000 for each qualified participant — and deduct this amount as a current operating expense. For highly-compensated employees, this becomes a quite significant tax deduction for the business.

An employer (owner) may sponsor any number of retirement plans — of any type — that he chooses. The overall upper limit of his deductible contributions to all such plans, however, is 25% of a participant's compensation. It is conceivable, therefore, that an aggressive owner could rig his business affairs in such a way that a good portion of his own compensation was tax deferred. But this is highly unlikely. Since all employees — owners and nonowners alike — must be eligible to participate, economic and administrative reality soon sets in.

EBSA Form 5500 for Each Plan

For practical reasons, the limit in number of retirement plans that a business can sustain is three. These three plans are of the following types:

1. Pension plans: fixed contributions
2. Profit-sharing plans: variable contributions
3. Other plans: elective contributions

Each plan that is established and funded is a separate tax accountable entity on its own. Each plan must have its own separate EIN. This means that, for each plan, an annual information return has to be filed. The particular filing required is EBSA Form 5500: *Annual Return/Report of Employee Benefit Plan*. It is filed with the *Employee Benefits Security Administration* (EBSA), a division of the U.S. Department of Labor in Lawrence, Kansas. The EBSA is an affiliate of the Pension Benefit Guaranty Corporation. It is significant to note that Form 5500 is **not** filed with the IRS.

Form 5500, without any schedules attached, is a 4-page document accompanied by 68 pages of instructions. Of its 12 possible schedules, usually only about three are required for "small plans," meaning: *with fewer than 100 participants.*

Other than a plan's EIN, and the employer's (or sponsor's) EIN, the four pages of general information focus on—

    A. Number of participants at beginning of plan year _____
    B. Number of participants at end of plan year who are—

       ☐ Active _____   ☐ Retired _____

       ☐ Deceased (with beneficiaries receiving benefits ____

       ☐ Terminated (with benefits less than 100% vested) ____

    C. Plan assets and liabilities _____
    D. Current year income and expenses _____
    E. Benefits paid (including direct rollovers _____
    F. Specific asset values: ___ *(list each asset and its value)* ___

This asset/participant information is followed by two key reminders that:

(1) The plan must not hold more than 20% of its assets in any single security, debt, mortgage, parcel of real estate, or investment venture, and

(2) The plan must benefit at least 70% of employees who are not highly compensated.

Obviously, these two provisions are designed to prohibit an owner from stacking a plan solely in his favor.

We have intended the above to convey a subliminal message to you. The message is that the setup, funding, and maintenance of one or more retirement plans (pension, profit sharing, or elective deferral) for you **and** for your employees, are administratively complex . . . and financially draining. As a result, for a new business starting up — whether proprietorship, partnership, LLC, S corporation, or C corporation — we strongly urge that you **not** engage in such plans until after three full years of profitable business operations. You have to make money first, before you can stash any of it away for retirement.

ABOUT

THE AUTHOR

Holmes F. Crouch

Born on a small farm in southern Maryland, Holmes was graduated from the U.S. Coast Guard Academy with a Bachelor's Degree in Marine Engineering. While serving on active duty, he wrote many technical articles on maritime matters. After attaining the rank of Lieutenant Commander, he resigned to pursue a career as a nuclear engineer.

Continuing his education, he earned a Master's Degree in Nuclear Engineering from the University of California. He also authored two books on nuclear propulsion. As a result of the tax write-offs associated with writing these books, the IRS audited his returns. The IRS's handling of the audit procedure so annoyed Holmes that he undertook to become as knowledgeable as possible regarding tax procedures. He became a licensed private Tax Practitioner by passing an examination administered by the IRS. Having attained this credential, he started his own tax preparation and counseling business in 1972.

In the early years of his tax practice, he was a regular talk-show guest on San Francisco's KGO Radio responding to hundreds of phone-in tax questions from listeners. He was a much sought-after guest speaker at many business seminars and taxpayer meetings. He also provided counseling on special tax problems, such as divorce matters, property exchanges, timber harvesting, mining ventures, animal breeding, independent contractors, selling businesses, and offices-at-home. Over the past 25 years, he has prepared well over 10,000 tax returns for individuals, estates, trusts, and small businesses (in partnership and corporate form).

During the tax season of January through April, he prepares returns in a unique manner. During a single meeting, he completes the return . . . *on the spot!* The client leaves with his return signed, sealed, and in a stamped envelope. His unique approach to preparing returns and his personal interest in his clients' tax affairs have honed his professional proficiency. His expertise extends through itemized deductions, computer-matching of income sources, capital gains and losses, business expenses and cost of goods, residential rental expenses, limited and general partnership activities, closely-held corporations, to family farms and ranches.

He remembers spending 12 straight hours completing a doctor's complex return. The next year, the doctor, having moved away, utilized a large accounting firm to prepare his return. Their accountant was so impressed by the manner in which the prior return was prepared that he recommended the doctor travel the 500 miles each year to have Holmes continue doing it.

He recalls preparing a return for an unemployed welder, for which he charged no fee. Two years later the welder came back and had his return prepared. He paid the regular fee . . . and then added a $300 tip.

During the off season, he represents clients at IRS audits and appeals. In one case a shoe salesman's audit was scheduled to last three hours. However, after examining Holmes' documentation it was concluded in 15 minutes with "no change" to his return. In another instance he went to an audit of a custom jeweler that the IRS dragged out for more than six hours. But, supported by Holmes' documentation, the client's return was accepted by the IRS with "no change."

Then there was the audit of a language translator that lasted two full days. The auditor scrutinized more than $1.25 million in gross receipts, all direct costs, and operating expenses. Even though all expensed items were documented and verified, the auditor decided that more than $23,000 of expenses ought to be listed as capital items for depreciation instead. If this had been enforced it would have resulted in a significant additional amount of tax. Holmes strongly disagreed and after many hours explanation got the amount reduced by more than 60% on behalf of his client.

He has dealt extensively with gift, death and trust tax returns. These preparations have involved him in the tax aspects of wills, estate planning, trustee duties, probate, marital and charitable bequests, gift and death exemptions, and property titling.

Although not an attorney, he prepares Petitions to the U.S. Tax Court for clients. He details the IRS errors and taxpayer facts by citing pertinent sections of tax law and regulations. In a recent case involving an attorney's ex-spouse, the IRS asserted a tax deficiency of $155,000. On behalf of his client, he petitioned the Tax Court and within six months the IRS conceded the case.

Over the years, Holmes has observed that the IRS is not the industrious, impartial, and competent federal agency that its official public imaging would have us believe.

He found that, at times, under the slightest pretext, the IRS has interpreted against a taxpayer in order to assess maximum penalties, and may even delay pending matters so as to increase interest due on additional taxes. He has confronted the IRS in his own behalf on five separate occasions, going before the U.S. Claims Court, U.S. District Court, and U.S. Tax Court. These were court actions that tested specific sections of the Internal Revenue Code which he found ambiguous, inequitable, and abusively interpreted by the IRS.

Disturbed by the conduct of the IRS and by the general lack of tax knowledge by most individuals, he began an innovative series of taxpayer-oriented Federal tax guides. To fulfill this need, he undertook the writing of a series of guidebooks that provide in-depth knowledge on one tax subject at a time. He focuses on subjects that plague taxpayers all throughout the year. Hence, his formulation of the "Allyear" Tax Guide series.

The author is indebted to his wife, Irma Jean, and daughter, Barbara MacRae, for the word processing and computer graphics that turn his experiences into the reality of these publications. Holmes welcomes comments, questions, and suggestions from his readers. He can be contacted in California at (408) 867-2628, or by writing to the publisher's address.

ALLYEAR Tax Guides
by Holmes F. Crouch

For information about the above titles, contact
Holmes F. Crouch

Allyear Tax Guides

Phone: (408) 867-2628   Fax: (408) 867-6466